Library of
Davidson College

Handbook of criterion-referenced testing

Handbook of criterion-referenced testing:

development, evaluation, and use

Marion F. Shaycoft
American Institutes for Research
in the Behavioral Sciences
Palo Alto, California

GARLAND STPM PRESS
New York & London

We are grateful for permission to use the following copyrighted material: pp. 6 and 26-27 from *Educational Measurement,* © 1951, reprinted by permission of the American Council on Education; pp. 7-8 from *Educational and Psychological Measurement,* © 1962, reprinted by permission of *Educational and Psychological Measurement* and Robert Ebel; p. 14 from paper by Willard G. Warrington, presented 1970, printed here by permission of Willard G. Warrington; pp. 24-25 from *Educational Technology,* © 1972, reprinted by permission of Educational Technology Publications, Inc.; pp. 80-81 from Popham, W. J., & Husek, T. R., "Implications of Criterion Referenced Measurement." *Journal of Educational Measurement,* 1969, Vol. 6, pp. 1-9. Copyright 1969, National Council on Measurement in Education, Inc., East Lansing, Michigan. Reprinted by special permission; p. 90 adapted from *Psychometrika,* © 1953, by permission of Psychometric Society and William Angoff.

Copyright © 1979 by American Institutes for Research in the Behavioral Sciences, Inc.

The work presented herein was performed pursuant to a contract from the U.S. Office of Education, Department of Health, Education, and Welfare. However, the opinions expressed herein do not necessarily reflect the position or policy of the U.S. Office of Education, and no official endorsement by the U.S. Office of Education should be inferred.

All rights reserved. No part of this work covered by the copyright hereon may be reproduced or used in any form or by any means—graphic, electronic, or mechanical, including photocopying, recording, taping, or information storage and retrieval systems—without permission of the publisher.

Library of Congress Cataloging in Publication Data

Shaycoft, Marion F. 1917–
    Handbook of criterion-referenced testing.

    Bibliography: p.
    Includes index.
    1. Educational tests and measurements. I. Title.
LB3051.S46   371.2'6   78-20643
ISBN 0-8240-7060-7

15 14 13 12 11 10 9 8 7 6 5 4 3 2 1

Published by Garland STPM Press, 545 Madison Avenue,
New York, New York 10022

Printed in the United States of America

Contents

List of Tables, xi
List of Figures and Exhibits, xiii
Acknowledgments, xv

1. INTRODUCTION   1

PURPOSE OF THIS BOOK, 1
DEFINITION OF BASIC TERMS, 2
  Norm-referenced test, 3
  Criterion-referenced test, 3
    Domain-referenced measurement, 4
    Objective-referenced measurement, 4
HISTORICAL ANTECEDENTS OF THE CRITERION-
    REFERENCED TEST, 5
OVERVIEW OF THIS BOOK, 8

2. THE RELATION OF CRITERION-REFERENCED
TESTS TO TESTS OF OTHER KINDS   9

CLASSIFICATION OF ACHIEVEMENT TESTS IN
    TERMS OF PURPOSE, 9
  Achievement tests and predictive tests, 9
  Can a predictive test be criterion-referenced? 10
  Can a test be both criterion-referenced and norm-
    referenced at the same time? 11
CLASSIFICATION OF CRITERION-REFERENCED
    TESTS IN TERMS OF MODALITY OF TEST AND
    NATURE OF CRITERION, 13
  Non-paper-and-pencil tests, 13
  Paper-and-pencil tests, 13
    Objective-referenced tests, 13
    Domain-referenced tests, 15
SUMMARY, 16

3. DEVELOPING CRITERION-REFERENCED TESTS FOR MEASURING SCHOOL ACHIEVEMENT   17

PLANNING PHASE, 17
DEFINING WHAT IS TO BE MEASURED, 18
   Defining the domain (for domain-referenced tests), 19
   Defining the objective or objectives (for objective-referenced tests), 22
TEST RATIONALES, 28
SAMPLING FROM THE DOMAIN, 29
WRITING THE TEST ITEMS, 37
   Item type, 38
   Item writing, 38
TRYOUT AND ITEM ANALYSIS, 50
   For domain-referenced tests, 50
   For objective-referenced tests, 51
   General considerations, 53

4. NORMS   56

   NEED FOR NORMS, 56
   HOW TO DEVELOP NORMS FOR CRITERION-REFERENCED TESTS, 56
   HOW TO USE NORMS FOR CRITERION-REFERENCED TESTS, 59

5. USING CRITERION-REFERENCED TESTS   61

   CATEGORIES OF USES OF CRITERION-REFERENCED TESTS, 61
      Evaluation of status, 61
         To evaluate the achievement of individuals or groups for diagnostic purposes (formative evaluation), 61
         Overall evaluation of the achievement of individuals or groups (summative evaluation), 61
      Evaluation of change, 65
   SETTING THE STANDARD OF COMPETENCE, 65

The concept of "standard of competence," 65
How the standard of competence is set: the role
  of norms, 67
The "mastery level" concept, 69
SETTING THE CUTTING SCORE, 70
SITUATIONS WHERE REPEATED TESTINGS
  ARE REQUIRED, 72
Evaluation of an educational program, method, or
  curriculum, 72
Other situations requiring repeated testing, 72
Handling repeated testing, 72
Effect on teaching: the teaching-to-the-test problem, 74
USING CRITERION-REFERENCED TESTS FOR
  FORMATIVE AND SUMMATIVE EVALUATIONS, 74
Formative evaluations, 74
Summative evaluations, 75
  Summative evaluations of individuals and groups, 75
  *Evaluation of an innovative program or
    curriculum,* 75
SCORING MULTIPLE-CHOICE TESTS, 76

6. EVALUATING CRITERION-REFERENCED TESTS 80

RELIABILITY, 86
For tests to be used in a school-related context, 86
  General considerations, 86
  Recommended procedure, 86
For evaluation of individuals (in or out of school) with
  respect to a particular domain, 90
A procedure that is *not* recommended for reliability
  estimation, 90
VALIDITY, 91
Validation for evaluating the achievement of individuals
  or groups, 92
Validation of a criterion-referenced test for use
  in evaluating the effectiveness of an educational
  program, 93
Predictive validity, 93

ACCURACY, 94
  General characteristics of accuracy statistics, 95
  Coefficient of accuracy, 96
    Comparison with reliability coefficients, 96
    Comparison with Livingston's "reliability coefficient," 96
  Evaluation of the usefulness of the coefficient of accuracy (and the other accuracy statistics), 98

7. SUMMARY   100

SCOPE AND CONTENT, 101
DEFINITIONS OF BASIC TERMS, 101
  Criterion-referenced tests, 101
  Kinds of criterion-referenced tests, 101
    Domain-referenced measurement, 102
    Objective-referenced measurement, 102
  Behavioral objectives, 102
SHATTERED ICONS, 102
SUGGESTIONS ON APPROACHES AND PROCEDURES, 111
  Developing criterion-referenced tests, 111
    Objectives, 111
    Test rationales, 112
    Sampling the domain, 112
    Writing the items, 112
    Tryout and item analysis, 113
  Norms for criterion-referenced tests, 113
  Using criterion-referenced tests, 113
    Relation between what is tested, what is taught, and what the objectives are, 113
    Cutting scores and standards of competence, 114
    Repeated testings, 114
    Scoring multiple-choice criterion-referenced tests, 115
  Evaluating criterion-referenced tests, 115
    Reliability, 115
      Suggested procedures, 115

Comments on the Livingston procedure, 116
Validation of criterion-referenced tests, 116
  For evaluating the achievement of individuals or groups, 116
  For evaluating the effectiveness of an educational program, 116
"Accuracy statistics," 116
A FINAL WORD, 117

References, 118

Appendix A. A Paradox In Setting Cutting Scores on Criterion-referenced Tests — 122

THE PROBLEM, 122
PERSPECTIVE AND THEORETICAL FRAMEWORK, 123
  Errors of measurement in criterion-referenced tests, 123
  Mathematical model, 124
RESULTS AND CONCLUSIONS, 153
EDUCATIONAL IMPORTANCE, 153

Appendix B. The "Accuracy Analogues" of Various Standard Statistics, 155

Index, 165

List of tables

Table 3-1. Stratified sampling of the content domain, for domain-referenced vocabulary test	32
Table 5-1. Some uses of criterion-referenced tests	62
Table 5-2. Relation of mastery of item sample constituting the test to mastery of population of items constituting the domain	66
Table 6-1. Uses of criterion-referenced tests, for which test evaluation may be needed	84
Table 6-2. Reliability coefficients and coefficients of accuracy for specified combinations of random error and systematic error	97
Table 7-1. Summary of prevalent fallacies discussed in this book	103
Table A-1. Demonstration of method of calculating theoretical distribution of scores (matrix x) on a criterion-referenced test with a specified number of items and a specified number of options per item for individuals at specified levels of competence	127
Table A-2. Theoretical distributions of scores on criterion-referenced test for individuals at specified levels of competence	
Table 2a. Constructed-answer Items	128
Table 2b. Five-choice Items	132
Table 2c. Four-choice Items	136
Table 2d. Three-choice Items	140
Table 2e. Two-choice Items	144
Table A-3. Proportion of cases at various levels of competence who would pass and proportion who would fail, with various cutting scores	148
Table A-4. Distributions indicating hypothetical percentages of population at various levels of competence, at five different stages	150
Table A-5. Percentage distribution of classification categories, at various stages with various kinds of tests and various cutting scores	151
Table A-6. Relative amount of misclassification at various stages with various cutting scores	152

Table B-1. Summary of notation used in Appendix B to represent variables 155

Table B-2. Standard formulas (for conventional statistics) and corresponding formulas for statistics referring to or dependent on absolute scores 162

List of figures and exhibits

Figure 1-1. Classification of tests in terms of test purpose and mode of score interpretation — 12

Exhibit 3-1. Examples of word meanings in each stratum of domain-referenced vocabulary test — 34

Exhibit 3-2. Construction of domain-referenced vocabulary test: Selecting the degree of specificity of knowledge to be tested — 40

Exhibit 3-3. Construction of domain-referenced vocabulary test: Illustrating the appropriate use of diagrams, and the inappropriate use of dictionary definitions — 44

Exhibit 3-4. Extracts from rationale for domain-referenced vocabulary test — 46

Exhibit A-1. Notation and formulas — 125

Acknowledgments

I am indebted to many people for their review of this book and their helpful suggestions; and also for their patience in letting me bounce ideas off of them. Among those to whom I owe a debt of gratitude are four of my past and present colleagues—John C. Flanagan, William V. Clemans, Daryl G. Nichols, and Albert B. Chalupsky—all of whom read the draft and made valuable suggestions.

Also among those to whom I am particularly indebted are three members of the United States Office of Education staff—Carl Wisler, George Mayeske, and Jan Anderson. I know that the book is substantially improved as a consequence of their suggestions.

Jason Millman, in a private communication, pointed out some similarities between the type of findings I reported in Table A-2a and a set of tables he constructed for the Instructional Objectives Exchange; one of his tables is also in his *Review of Educational Research* article (Millman, 1973). Although that table has a somewhat different purpose and therefore is considerably narrower in scope than the Appendix A table (Table A-2a), wherever there is overlap the two tables agree *exactly;* this is reassuring. I am grateful to Dr. Millman for his very kind comments on what is now Appendix A (but was, when he saw it, the manuscript for an AERA paper).

Some of the viewpoints expressed in the book differ considerably from the "conventional wisdom" about criterion-referenced tests. It goes without saying, but I shall say it anyway: I take full responsibility for any errors of fact or opinion that there may be in this book.

Marion F. Shaycoft

Handbook of criterion-referenced testing

1
Introduction

PURPOSE OF THIS BOOK

In the decade and a half since the concept of criterion-referenced measurement surfaced and impinged on the consciousness of educational researchers and test users in general, it has received widespread and enthusiastic attention from a rather large segment of the test-using community. Much of the enthusiasm is merited; criterion-referenced measurement with carefully developed instruments, used in an appropriate context, *can* perform a useful function. Unfortunately, however, there is an enormous amount of confusion about this type of measurement. In apparent obedience to a Gresham's law of psychometrics, the following misconceptions have all gained wide currency in recent years:

1. That criterion-referenced tests are innately superior to norm-referenced tests.

2. That "classical" psychometric theory is inapplicable to criterion-referenced tests.

3. That the concept of "reliability," in particular, is inapplicable.

4. That a criterion-referenced test cannot also be norm-referenced; and conversely that a norm-referenced test cannot be criterion-referenced.

5. That criterion-referenced tests should be substituted for norm-referenced tests in all contexts where the latter are now commonly used.

6. That "predictive tests" (tests intended to predict performance at some future time as indicated by an appropriate criterion measure) should be "criterion-referenced" in the sense in which that term is commonly used (in this book and elsewhere).

7. That in developing a criterion-referenced test the goal necessarily should be a test on which everyone in the group performs perfectly, or nearly perfectly.

None of the above notions has a sound factual basis. This book is addressed primarily to two groups: those who have acquired some or all of the misconceptions listed above, and those who have had so little experience with criterion-referenced tests or with the literature about them that they have not had time to acquire the misconceptions. It is hoped that members of a third group, consisting of those who are familiar with the prevalent misconceptions mentioned above and have been made uneasy by them, will agree with the viewpoint expressed and the approach advocated in this book.

Thus the purposes of this book are, in brief, to show how to decide whether a particular situation calls for a criterion-referenced test; how to develop (or select) such a test; how such a test should be evaluated; and what its proper uses are (and are not). To delimit the scope a little further, it should be pointed out that in this book we are concerned almost exclusively with *paper-and-pencil* criterion-referenced tests rather than performance tests, and also that we are focusing primarily on the use of tests in educational measurement.

DEFINITION OF BASIC TERMS

The terms criterion-referenced measurement, objective-referenced measurement, and domain-referenced measurement have been used more or less interchangeably by some writers, while others have attributed slightly different meanings to these three terms, and still others have used only one of the three terms to cover all the concepts with which they deal that are related to criterion-referenced measurement. Since there is no uniformity of usage and since there *is* a need for terms to express certain distinctions, we propose the following usage, which will be adhered to in the remainder of this book.

"Criterion-referenced measurement" is the general term under which the two main types, domain-referenced measurement and objective-referenced measurement, are subsumed. These two types will be defined and discussed in the next section. To understand criterion-referenced tests, we first have to understand norm-referenced measurement and norm-referenced tests.

Norm-referenced test

A person's score on a norm-referenced test is interpreted in terms of its relation to scores of the members of some appropriate, clearly defined group of which he may or may not be a member. For instance an English test that provided percentile norms for grades 6, 7, 8, and 9 based on a representative sample of all the sixth-, seventh-, eighth-, and ninth-graders in the United States would be norm-referenced. It would still be norm-referenced if the scale for converting raw scores to percentiles were based on a representative sample of a somewhat more restricted group—for instance seventh-graders in *public* schools only (rather than all kinds of schools having a seventh grade), in the six New England states only (rather than all over the country); or if the ninth-grade norms sample were restricted to students in a college-preparatory curriculum. A norm-referenced test might use some system of norming other than percentiles; for instance grade equivalents might be used although it should be pointed out that in the opinion of the present writer, and many others as well, the use of grade equivalents causes many more problems than it solves. See for instance Horst, Tallmadge, and Wood (1974, pp. 9–10) or Tallmadge and Horst (1974, pp. 79–92). There is also some further discussion of the matter in Chapter 4 of this book.

Norms provided by the test publisher—based on a sample from a general population of some sort—are sometimes supplemented by "local norms"; for example norms based on a particular school or school district and developed locally, by personnel from the school system. The distinctive characteristic of norm-referenced measurement is that scores are interpreted in terms of how the individual stands with respect to some appropriate larger group.

Criterion-referenced test

In criterion-referenced measurement—unlike norm-referenced measurement—scores are interpreted as having some sort of absolute meaning in terms, for instance, of level of performance or amount achieved or degree of mastery; in other words, the criterion-referenced score has some sort of meaning in itself, irrespective of the scores for specified groups.

There is no well-established standard usage for classifying or designating types of criterion-referenced measurement, but in this book we are using two main categories, which we are identifying by the terms "domain-referenced measurement" and "objective-referenced measurement."

Domain-referenced measurement

In a domain-referenced test the overall score has absolute meaning (criterion-referenced meaning) in the sense of indicating what proportion of some defined domain the examinee has mastered.[1] This type of measurement is most suitable when the area to be measured is a domain that can be clearly defined, the number of possible elements in it is within finite bounds, and a "sampling frame" listing all the elements of the domain exists or can be readily constructed, so that a probability sample of elements to be tested can be drawn from it.

Objective-referenced measurement

Objective-referenced measurement refers to the kind of test (or subtest) that corresponds to a specific objective of instruction or a specific objective that is to be achieved by the examinee. The test or subtest usually consists of a comparatively small number of items drawn from a larger set of possible items. Since the objective is usually *mastery* of some specific skill or acquisition of a quite specific piece of information the logical representation of the requisite mastery would be a perfect score. Most practitioners, however, find it too difficult to get all the students in a class to achieve this standard, and therefore in practice they usually settle for something less than perfection; perhaps for 90% correct. It might be mentioned in passing that this is an instance of using normative data as a basis for establishing the *standard* of performance (the "criterion score") on a criterion-referenced test. We shall have more to say later about this somewhat paradoxical practice.

Probably the chief way in which the two kinds of criterion-referenced measurement differ is in terms of the kind of score scales they are intended to yield. Domain-referenced measurement is designed to yield a continuous score scale in which a maximum score represents 100% mastery of the defined domain and a minimum score indicates total absence of mastery of any part of that domain. Objective-referenced measurement, on the other hand, usually yields just a dichotomous score that indicates whether the examinee has reached the designated standard of performance corresponding to the specified objective.

HISTORICAL ANTECEDENTS OF THE CRITERION-REFERENCED TEST

Criterion-referenced tests have their roots both in nonstandardized tests and in standardized tests. Regarding the former, the old-fashioned teacher-made tests with a passing mark set at some arbitrary percentage value, such as 65% or 70% or perhaps 75%, might in a loose sort of way be regarded as criterion-referenced tests— very poorly criterion-referenced, to be sure, but nevertheless widely thought to serve the same function as some criterion-referenced tests are now intended to serve. Although the tests with a set percentage as a passing mark were virtually never constructed in such a way as to systematically sample the content of a course (and if they were essay tests they were probably not scored in any standard manner), nevertheless the percentage score was often assumed to indicate the percentage of what had been taught that had been mastered.

Of course it generally indicated no such thing. The difficulty level, the nature of the sampling of the course content, and the scoring standards in such tests were sometimes erratic. But even when they were quite reasonable, they were not *standardized* in any way—certainly not in any way that would permit the attribution of absolute meaning to scores. A child who had in fact mastered 75% of the material taught in a particular subject (e.g. science) in a particular grade might easily get a score a lot higher or a lot lower than 75%, depending on the nature of the test and the scoring procedures.

As for their roots in *standardized* tests, it should be noted that some criterion-referenced tests have a strong resemblance to one of the three categories into which most norm-referenced tests have sometimes been classified—survey tests, prognostic tests, and diagnostic tests. "Survey tests" are norm-referenced tests used to provide an overall indication of where groups or the individuals in them stand in terms of general level of ability or achievement in a particular area. "Prognostic tests" are tests used for predictive purposes. And "diagnostic tests" are tests intended to provide not merely an overall score for each student but also a profile of the student's strengths and weaknesses in terms of specific topics and skills. Thus diagnostic tests bear a close resemblance, at least in purpose if not in manner of development, to many of today's criterion-referenced tests.

The term "criterion-referenced measurement" did not come into use until 1963, when Glaser (1963) coined it. But the concept existed long before that. As a matter of fact, fully a dozen years before, Flanagan (1951b) had stressed the difference between norms and standards, which is, of course, a crucial difference between norm-referencing and criterion-referencing. In this connection Flanagan said:

> Test "norms" may be defined as estimates of some characteristic of a distribution of test scores for a specified population. Norms describe the actual performance of specified groups of individuals. "Standards," on the other hand, are desirable, or desired, levels of attainment, preferably expressed in terms of outcomes of instruction. (1951b, p. 698)

And as far back as 1939 Flanagan had in essence described criterion-referenced tests, when he wrote:

> [One of the two] fundamental point[s] of reference in describing individual achievement concerns the performance of the individual with respect to the content of the test rather than the achievement of individuals or groups taking the test. Illustrative of this are such statements as, "This individual's score indicates that he probably knows the meanings of 9,000 of the 18,000 words of a particular dictionary," or ... "He can translate a typical page of Cicero making fewer than three errors...." The statement concerning the individual's vocabulary illustrates the method of an enumerative sample.... The statement concerning his ability to translate ... Cicero [indicates] attainment of a defined level on a "difficulty" scale. (Flanagan, 1939)

In the same document he described as one of the four main types of descriptive information obtainable from educational measurements:

> A description of an individual's performance expressed in terms which are absolute with respect to specific or defined functions and materials included in the test . . . in contrast to one which is relative to other individuals or groups. (Ibid.)

There were even some tests developed before the term "criterion-referenced test" had been coined that would be considered criterion-referenced by almost any standards. For instance, four criterion-referenced tests were developed in 1960 (one in vocabulary, one in spelling, and two in reading comprehension) for use in Project TALENT as an auxiliary to the regular TALENT test battery. These tests, which were conceived by Flanagan, were called "domain tests." The vocabulary test was designed to indicate how many word meanings from the unabridged dictionary (Merriam-Webster, Second Edition) the examinee knew. The score on the spelling test yielded an estimate of how many words he could spell, among the first 5000 most frequently appearing in print. One of the two reading comprehension tests measured comprehension of fiction (ten famous authors, arranged in order of the difficulty of prose), while the other measured comprehension of magazine articles (ten magazines with national circulation, also arranged in order of difficulty). These four "domain tests" are described by Shaycoft (1964 and 1968).[2] In the terminology used in this book they would be called "domain-referenced" tests.

Others too, besides Flanagan, preceded Glaser in recognizing the potential utility of tests in which raw scores would be meaningful in themselves, quite apart from any normative data. For instance Ebel (1962) advocated the development of what he called "content standard tests," which were essentially the same as what we are calling "domain-referenced" tests. He came straight to the point, by writing:

> It is unfortunate, I think, that some specialists in measuring educational achievement have seemed to imply that knowing how many of his peers a student can excel is more important than knowing what he can do to excel them. Note that we are not here objecting to invidious

comparisons nor supporting the allegation of psycho-social harm in competition. Our point is that when comparative scores are not clearly related to specific achievements they tend to have rather limited meaning and educational value.

To be meaningful any test scores must be related to test content as well as to the scores of other examinees. (Ebel, 1962)

OVERVIEW OF THIS BOOK

In this chapter we have said a little about different kinds of tests. In Chapter 2 we go into considerably more detail on this point, discussing not only what the different kinds are but whether and how they overlap. A fairly good idea of the content of Chapters 3, 4, 5, and 6 can be obtained by perusing the table of contents. (Chapters 1 and 2 are largely "background," while Chapters 3-6 provide "how-to" information.) Chapter 7 emphasizes the salient points from the preceding chapters and presents in brief form the viewpoint that has shaped this book.

This book is organized in a way designed to make information readily accessible, and it has a very detailed table of contents, in order to facilitate its possible use as a reference document. In an effort to keep the book as nontechnical as possible, strictly mathematical materials such as derivations of formulas have been relegated to appendixes.

NOTES

[1] Scores do not necessarily have to *equal* the proportion of the domain that the examinee has mastered, but in general they should at least be a linear function of that proportion.

[2] The 1964 reference describes the construction of the spelling and reading tests, and presents the results for them. The 1968 reference presents corresponding information for the vocabulary test.

2
The relation of criterion-referenced tests to tests of other kinds

As has already been indicated, many of the numerous misconceptions about criterion-referenced tests are founded in the seminal misconception that criterion-referenced and norm-referenced tests are two entirely different species, and ''never the twain shall meet.'' In this chapter we shall focus on this misconception.

CLASSIFICATION OF ACHIEVEMENT TESTS IN TERMS OF PURPOSE
Achievement tests and predictive tests

We have seen that one of the dimensions in which tests may differ is in the manner in which scores are interpreted. If the score scale is set up in such a way that each score has some sort of absolute meaning, quite independent of normative data, the test is criterion-referenced. By ''normative data'' as the term is used here, we mean any data concerning how well specific groups perform on the test. If scores are interpreted in terms of percentiles, or a standard score scale, or normalized standard scores, or any other way that depends directly on how the scores were distributed in a specific group or groups, the test is norm-referenced.

Both of these styles of interpretation can be applied to achievement tests. But the evaluation of the absolute or relative level of mastery that has been achieved is not the only purpose for which a test that measures past achievement might be administered. Sometimes such a test is used as a measure of aptitude—in other words as a predictor of future achievement. For instance a test measuring achievement in certain kinds of verbal and mathematical skills has been designed to be used as a predictor of success in college, and is therefore widely used by colleges as one basis for deciding which of the applicants will be admitted. We refer, of course, to the Scholastic Aptitude Test (SAT). What makes it an "aptitude test" rather than an achievement test is not its form or content but its purpose. Its purpose is not to measure past achievement but to predict future performance.

Can a predictive test be criterion-referenced?

Are predictive tests such as the SAT criterion-referenced or are they norm-referenced? Normative data are provided, of course. Indeed, they were built into the standard score scale, which was set up on the basis of the distribution of applicants' scores, to have a mean of 500 and a standard deviation of 100. In a sense, then, the test is norm-referenced. But the chief purpose of the test is to predict future achievement rather than to evaluate past achievement. Colleges would have little interest in scores on an achievement test in an area that had little or no predictive value for college success. For instance a test of skill in sewing might have very fine norms, and it might even be scored in such a way as to be "criterion-referenced"—if the criterion to which it was referenced were an indication of level of skill in sewing—but it would not be used as a college admission test, since there would be no reason to expect scores on it to be correlated with success in college. Thus, in the case of score on a predictive test, the critical thing is what the measurement it provides tells about the *future,* not the past or present.

Then does what it tells us about the likelihood of success in college make it a criterion-referenced test (assuming, of course, that success in college is the agreed-upon criterion)? No, not really. The score in itself has no absolute meaning with respect to success in college. A score above 750 may suggest (on normative grounds) that a student is capable of A-level work at a highly selective college, but there is nothing intrinsic in the score itself to equate it with grades of A in college courses. There *would* be such an intrinsic relation only if the professor assigning grades in a particular course were to consider the content of the SAT to coincide with what he was teaching in his course and to consider the SAT "achievement level" represented by a score of 750 to be A-level work in the course. *Predicting* A-level work is not enough; the SAT "achievement level" would have to *be* A-level work, by definition, for the SAT to be considered criterion-referenced.

In summary, then, the concept of criterion-referenced measurement is applicable to evaluative measurement (e.g. achievement tests) but seldom, if ever, to predictive tests. Conceivably, standards of achievement on an achievement test (whether norm-referenced or criterion-referenced) can be set that will be predictive of success in whatever future activity one is trying to predict success in—but even in that case it is the criterion of success in the predicted activity that is important, not an arbitrary standard of success on the criterion-referenced test itself. To show the validity of such a use of a criterion-referenced test, it would therefore be necessary to validate it against whatever criterion one has of success in the future activity. Pending the collection of such criterion data, one might appeal to the "construct validity" of the criterion-referenced test—but that would be tantamount to using the objective or domain on which the criterion-referenced test was based as a proximal criterion for success in the activity being predicted. (Validation against a proximal criterion is at best an interim measure—never a substitute for eventual validation against a more relevant criterion.)

Can a test be both criterion-referenced and norm-referenced at the same time?

Of course a test can be both norm-referenced and criterion-referenced. It is not as if norm-referencing and criterion-referencing were at opposite ends of the same dimension. They aren't. Rather, they constitute two entirely distinct dimensions. Ebel (1973), Angoff (1974), Mattson (1970), Warrington (1970), and other authorities have all pointed out, in effect, that criterion-referenced and norm-referenced tests are not mutually exclusive concepts. As An-

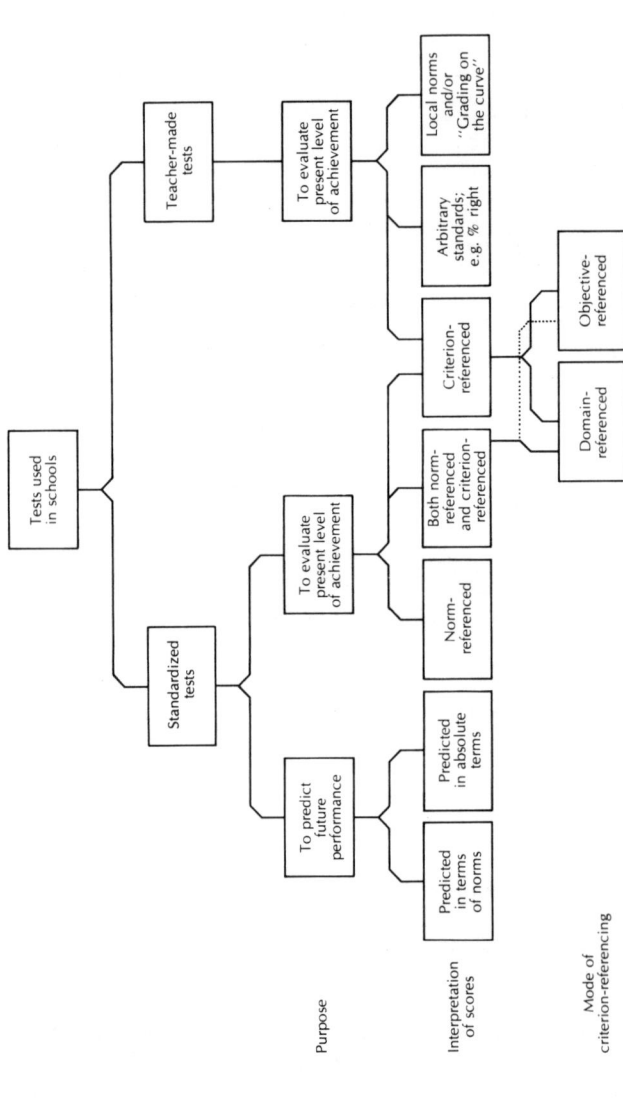

Figure 1-1. Classification of tests in terms of test purpose and mode of score interpretation. (Use of a dotted line is intended to suggest that, as is pointed out in Chapter 4, norm-referencing is necessarily somewhat more limited in scope for an objective-referenced test than for a domain-referenced test.)

goff (1974) says, "If you scratch a criterion-referenced interpretation, you will very likely find a norm-referenced set of assumptions underneath."

Figure 1-1 shows how the various sorts of tests are classified in terms of test purpose and mode of score interpretation.

CLASSIFICATION OF CRITERION-REFERENCED TESTS IN TERMS OF MODALITY OF TEST AND NATURE OF CRITERION

Non-paper-and-pencil tests

Criterion-referenced tests are not restricted to paper-and-pencil instruments. In fact performance batteries of various kinds, not involving paper-and-pencil tests, may be among the oldest types of criterion-referenced tests.

Consider skill with a rifle, for instance. A score scale might be established in terms of how close one's shots are to the center of the bull's-eye. Suppose, for instance, that one's score, shooting from a distance of 200 yards, is set equal to the average distance of one's shots from the center of the bull's-eye. (The better the marksman, the lower the score.) That would certainly be a criterion-referenced score since one's score would have a very definite meaning in terms of an absolute scale of performance, without reference to how one compared to other people. Since the topic of interest here, however, is criterion-referenced measurement in education, the remainder of this book is concerned primarily with paper-and-pencil tests.

Paper-and-pencil tests

Objective-referenced tests

In the educational context, criterion-referenced tests are most often used as end-of-year, end-of-semester, end-of-course, end-of-unit, or end-of-module achievement tests. These are very often of the objective-referenced type dichotomizing the group into those who have met the objective within the specified tolerance (e.g. 95% of the items correct) and those who have not—in other words a simple pass-fail dichotomization. As Warrington (1970) points out convincingly, dichotomization is usually undesirable, because it throws away information. He says:

> Even when time is a variable, individual differences in the quality of learning will certainly exist. Surely not all students who can successfully accomplish even a simple task at a rate of 95% correctness have identical learning of the concepts necessary to accomplish that task. It would, therefore, seem better to have some variety in the difficulty level of the mastery test that would thus provide some discrimination within the group, which should be helpful in designing subsequent learning activities. I see no reason why a minimum cut-off could not be specified which would indicate mastery and readiness for new learning, while at the same time the distance of the score above or below the cutoff would provide additional data about the individual learner.

If Warrington's suggestion were widely adopted (as we think it would be useful to do) it would wipe out, or at least make less clear-cut, part of the distinction we have been making between objective-referenced and domain-referenced measurement, but that is not important. The accuracy of the conclusions drawn would be substantially improved if the cases were not crudely dichotomized at an essentially arbitrary point.

Limiting output from an objective-referenced test to the mere information that one has, or has not, met a specific objective in terms of a standard such as 90% correct (which presumably has been quite as arbitrarily established as the old-fashioned "passing mark" of 70%), is restrictive and unnecessary.

There is no circumstance in which a dichotomous score scale is likely to provide more information than a continuous scale, and in most cases it will provide considerably less. In a conventional norm-referenced test the range of possible test scores should make it possible to differentiate among the members of a group—high scores indicating relatively high ability or achievement levels and low scores indicating relatively low levels. Likewise, for criterion-referenced tests the range of possible scores should indicate different levels of mastery of the skill or acquisition of the knowledge that corresponds to the entity being measured. A score of zero (or in the case of multiple-choice tests or tests in some other objective format, a score corresponding to chance success) should indicate lack of progress toward mastery of the objective or lack of mastery of any portion of the domain. Likewise, a perfect score on a criterion-referenced test, or on that portion of it corresponding to a specific objective, should indicate achievement of the objective within whatever standards have been established.

Domain-referenced tests

Domain-referenced tests, in the sense in which we are using the term, may or may not be usable as end-of-unit or end-of-module achievement tests; it depends on their content. A domain-referenced test, it will be recalled, is one in which the overall score has absolute meaning (criterion-referenced meaning) in a numerical sense, and quite beyond the dichotomous information provided by the typical objective-referenced test.

The following are examples of the kinds of information that might be derived from domain-referenced tests:

1. How many meanings of adjectives are in one's recognition vocabulary.

The domain for this test could be defined as all adjectival meanings of all adjectives in the *American Heritage Dictionary of the English Language*. The test could then consist of multiple-choice items testing understanding of a probability sample of the meanings.

2. How many of the standard punctuation rules one has mastered well enough to permit one to apply them correctly.

The domain for this test would be the list of all the standard punctuation rules for the English language. This list is probably short enough that it would be unnecessary to sample them. An item corresponding to each rule could be written.

3. How many of the 5000 words that are the most common in printed materials one can write from dictation without misspelling.

The domain for this would be the list of all words in the first 5000 on the basis of frequency, in the Thorndike-Lorge list of word frequencies.

4. How well one can add two nonzero integers at least one of which has two digits and neither of which has more than two digits.

The domain for this test would consist of 8910 pairs of numbers meeting the above description. (The same two numbers in different order would be treated as two separate pairs.) For the test a probability sample of the 8910 pairs of numbers would be drawn.

For the first of the four possible domain-referenced tests listed above (the vocabulary test), the domain-referenced score (number of adjectival meanings understood) would have very little meaning apart from whatever normative data might be available. Domain-referenced scores on the other three tests, however, might provide rather useful information in certain contexts. For instance, from the score on the spelling test one might be able to make a reasonable estimate of how many spelling errors the examinee would be likely to make in writing a few pages of ordinary prose.

SUMMARY

The following are the main points made in this chapter:

1. A test can be both norm-referenced and criterion-referenced simultaneously.

2. An achievement test, whether norm-referenced or criterion-referenced or both, can also be used for predictive purposes.

3. However, if a criterion-referenced test is used for prediction, in that capacity it is almost certainly not functioning as a criterion-referenced instrument since the scores are not referenced to the appropriate criterion (the criterion to be predicted).

4. Even in the case of objective-referenced tests, it is better to use a continuous scale than a dichotomous scale in scoring, since the continuous scale provides more information.

5. It is possible to develop domain-referenced tests that in certain contexts have useful absolute meanings quite apart from whatever normative data, if any, may be available.

3
Developing criterion-referenced tests for measuring school achievement

Developing a criterion-referenced test is not as different from developing a norm-referenced test as is sometimes supposed. Before a test—any test—can be written, its general nature has to be planned and the specific domain, or the specific objectives, in regard to which ability or achievement is to be assessed must be determined. Thus both kinds of test require an extensive planning phase before the actual writing of the test is undertaken; and essentially the same principles are followed in actually writing the items. The widely held misconception that "behavioral objectives" are the earmark of a criterion-referenced test is just that—a misconception. Behavioral objectives are quite as likely to underlie a test that is considered to be norm-referenced as one that is intended to be criterion-referenced.

Thus a substantial part of this chapter applies to achievement tests in general rather than just to criterion-referenced tests. But there *are* some special problems in developing a good criterion-referenced test that do not apply to norm-referenced tests in general. (The converse is not true, since criterion-referenced tests are best viewed as a special kind of norm-referenced test rather than as an entirely different species.)

PLANNING PHASE

In planning a test, it is necessary, of course, to bear in mind the test's purpose, and the area to be covered. First and foremost, in considering the test's purpose, how it is to be used, we have to decide whether a criterion-referenced test is what is needed or whether a plain old-fashioned norm-referenced test with no pretensions to criterion-referencing will serve our purposes equally well or better. If at this point we decide in favor of criterion-referencing, the same considerations that led to that decision will also make it clear which of the two principal *kinds* of criterion-referenced test—the domain-referenced type or the objective-referenced type—is the appropriate one.

If a domain-referenced test is to be developed it will be necessary to define the domain very explicitly and very precisely; likewise, if an objective-referenced test is what is needed the objectives will require precise definition. As was implied in Chapter 2, if the concept of a sharp dichotomy between those who meet an objective (set in terms of percentage of items to be answered correctly) and those who fail to do so is abandoned in favor of recognition that there is not likely to be a precise cutting point below which all scores are equally unsatisfactory and above which all scores are equally satisfactory, the objective-referenced type of test tends to merge with the domain-referenced type. Definition of domain or objectives is discussed in the next section.

The general nature of the test, in terms of the amount of time it will require and the nature and approximate number of items it will include, should not be decided upon even tentatively until the domain (or objective) to be measured has been defined very explicitly so that there is no ambiguity whatever concerning the function of the test. The link between the objectives to be measured and the test that measures them is the test rationale. This is discussed later in this chapter.

It is also necessary to decide how many forms of the test should be developed. If multiple administrations of the test to the same examinee are contemplated (for instance if the test is to be used in a situation that requires both pretest and posttest data), more than one form will almost certainly have to be constructed. (This is discussed further in Chapter 5.)

DEFINING WHAT IS TO BE MEASURED

Although the distinction is really not a very sharp one, and in some sense is an artificial one, nevertheless in this section we find it advantageous to treat domain-referenced and objective-referenced tests separately since the formal procedures are a little different.

Defining the domain
(for domain-referenced tests)

In defining the domain to be measured by a domain-referenced test it is necessary to be extremely explicit. Suppose, for example, a domain-referenced vocabulary test is to be constructed, scores on which are to be convertible into numerical estimates of the size of a person's vocabulary. Once the decision to develop such a test has been made, the first step is to define the universe. In explaining how one goes about this, we shall use as an example a domain-referenced vocabulary test that was developed back in 1960[1]—before the terms "criterion-referenced test" and "domain-referenced test" had even been coined. The problems that had to be solved in developing the test typify the complexities encountered in defining a domain. Among the questions that had to be answered were the following:

What kinds of words should be included?

1. Should the universe be all-inclusive or should it be defined to exclude specialized technical words that appear only in an unabridged dictionary (e.g. "chamoisite")?
2. And what about words so specialized and so technical that they do not appear in any general dictionary—not even an unabridged one? (An example would be the statistical term "heteroscedastic.")
3. Should dialect words be included (e.g. "afeared")?
4. Should other words classified as illiterate (e.g. "ain't") be included?
5. Archaic words (e.g. "natheless")?
6. Colloquial words (e.g. "enthuse")?
7. Contractions (e.g. "didn't," "won't")?
8. Slang (e.g. "funky")?
9. Words generally considered profane or obscene?
10. Proper nouns (e.g. "Spaniard")?
11. Proper adjectives (e.g. "French")?
12. Names of historical persons (e.g. Jefferson)?
13. Names of fictional characters (e.g. Lancelot)?
14. Variant spellings?

15. Scottish words (e.g. "jo," "sleekit," "agley," "bairn")?
16. Foreign words (e.g. "adios")?
17. Multiword expressions (e.g. "heir apparent," "out of commission")?

It was decided to exclude from the defined domain all but the first of the 17 categories listed above.

Should the units constituting the domain be words or word meanings?

This question arises because many words, particularly relatively common ones, have more than one meaning. The word "stock," for instance, has 56 separate meanings in current usage, according to the *American Heritage Dictionary of the English Language* (44 as a noun, 3 as a transitive verb, 2 as an intransitive verb, 6 as an adjective, and 1 as an adverb. Should "stock" be considered one word or 56? From one viewpoint it can be considered 56 different words that happen to be spelled identically, rather than one word. Here are some sentences showing a few of the different meanings.

1. He had 15 shares of oil stock.
2. Chicken stock was a major ingredient of the soup.
3. He comes from European stock.
4. The drugstore keeps several brands in stock.
5. She acted in summer stock.
6. Rag-content paper stock was used.
7. The Puritans used stocks as a punishment device.
8. There are three stock mares on his farm.

These meanings are sufficiently different that it is reasonable to consider them functionally different words.

What does it mean to say that someone knows what the word "stock" (or any other multimeaning word) means? Does it mean that he knows at least one meaning (*any* one meaning)? or that he knows one meaning specified in advance? that he knows the easiest meaning? the most frequent meaning? the hardest meaning? a meaning about midway in difficulty between the easiest and the hardest? or a majority of the meanings? or all the meanings? This dilemma was resolved by the decision that the domain would be defined to consist of the meanings of the words, rather than the words themselves (e.g. the combination of letters s-t-o-c-k). In other words the elements of the domain would be semantic-orthographic, rather than purely orthographic. Each numbered definition for a given word and each part of speech was a separate entry in the sampling. Thus a word with 56 separate meanings would have about 56 times as many chances of being included in the sample as a word for which only one meaning is given.

What dictionary or other source document should be used to provide the population of word meanings?

The first question in this connection was whether to use a dictionary at all, or instead to use some sort of frequency sampling such as would have been provided by *The Teacher's Word Book of 30,000 Words* (Thorndike and Lorge, 1944). The decision was to use a dictionary.

The next decision that had to be made was what specific dictionary should be used. Should it be unabridged or would a "collegiate level" abridged dictionary (about 100,000–150,000 words) serve the purpose? What about a pocket dictionary (about 25,000 words)? The decision was to use the Merriam-Webster unabridged dictionary. (It was the second edition, incidentally; the third was not out at the time construction of the test was undertaken.)

Is the focus of concern to be comprehension of the spoken *or* printed *word?*

The decision was that the test would be concerned with comprehension of the *printed* word, not the spoken word. The fact that an examinee could answer a certain question correctly would mean that he understands the word when he encounters it in written form; but this was understood to be no guarantee that he would understand it in its spoken form. In fact there is a rather good chance that he may not, if the word is one that is pronounced quite differently from the way its spelling would suggest—"indict," for instance.

*What level of understanding and mastery
should the test scores indicate?*

In connection with this problem it was decided that the test should measure ability to comprehend words, "recognition vocabulary," and that no effort would be made to measure "recall vocabulary" (sometimes called "active vocabulary"). In line with this purpose of the test—to measure recognition rather than recall, the ability to comprehend the writing of others rather than the ability to express oneself in writing—"understanding of a word meaning" was considered to mean understanding at a fairly gross level. Very fine differentiations in meaning or implication were not a matter of concern. Knowing the answer to an item in this test would certainly not be considered a guarantee that the person would *use* the word appropriately. The most that a test item would be expected to measure would be whether the examinee has a reasonably accurate understanding of the meaning that the word is intended to convey.

Five specific problems (kinds of words to be included, what to do about multimeaning words, what source document to use, what level of understanding and mastery to measure, and whether the word is to be presented in writing or orally) that were encountered in defining the domain that would be used in developing the domain-referenced vocabulary test have been indicated above, and the decisions that were arrived at have been described. The important point, however, is not *what* decisions were made, but the fact that the decisions *were* made—in other words that the problem was treated in sufficient depth that the questions indicated above were raised, considered, and resolved; the decisions were made explicitly, not by default.

Defining the objective or objectives
(for objective-referenced tests)

In recent years there has been widespread emphasis on the use of "behavioral objectives" for instruction. The following is an example of a behavioral objective in algebra:

> To be able to solve quadratic equations that have integral coefficients.

Developing criterion-referenced tests

The following slightly longer statement might be regarded as clearer and better by some (although it really does not change the meaning at all, since the added clause is implicit in the shorter version above):

> To be able to solve quadratic equations that have integral coefficients, regardless of whether the two solutions are equal or different, integral or fractional (or one of each), positive or negative (or one of each), rational or irrational, real or complex.

Note that implicit in either version of the statement of the behavioral objective is a corresponding universe of quadratic equations; the universe is infinite, since no restriction has been placed on the coefficients except that they must be integers.

Note also that implicit in the statement of the behavioral objective is the kind of test items that should be used to determine whether the objective has been achieved. The most direct way of testing whether this has occurred is by giving the students a set of quadratic equations to solve. The set should include all possible kinds of answers (i.e. both solutions positive, both solutions negative, one of each, both solutions complex, integral answers, fractional answers, etc.).

According to many of those at the forefront of the behavioral objectives movement, the behavioral statement should not just imply what the test items *will be like*; it should incorporate a statement concerning what proportion of the items the examinee *must answer correctly* in order to be deemed to have achieved "mastery." For instance according to this very prevalent belief the quadratic-equation objective might be expanded to the following:

> To be able to solve 7 out of 10 quadratic equations with integral coefficients, that have same-sign real-integer solutions, 7 out of 10 that have mixed-sign real-integer solutions, 7 out of 10 that have at least one rational fractional solution, 7 out of 10 that have irrational solutions, and 7 out of 10 whose solutions are complex numbers.

It is the opinion of the author of this book and of many others as well, for instance Wight (1972), that this sort of thing confuses objectives (i.e. goals, aims, aspirations) with minimum standards. No teacher worth his salt should be willing to regard 70% (or even

80%, for that matter) as mastery. It may be the best that can be expected from some students, but those students have not truly mastered the skill. The dictionary definition of mastery (*American Heritage Dictionary of the English Language*) is "possession of consummate skill." In any fairly representative group there will be some students who *can* achieve mastery, some who can come fairly close, and many who will learn just enough to achieve a borderline passing mark (wherever the passing mark may be set) and will then proceed to forget rapidly what they have learned.

Consider the road test and the multiple-choice information test that many states administer to applicants for a driver's license. The *objective* of the test is to keep unsafe drivers off the road. If the passing mark on the multiple-choice test is 85% correct, that is the *standard* that is set, *not* the objective. Surely the authorities would prefer that candidates score closer to 100%.

Wight (1972) zeroes in on some of the weaknesses of behavioral objectives with respect to the terms in which they are framed and the manner in which they are currently used:

> The problem of triviality and most other problems with behavioral objectives are a direct result of a means versus ends type of confusion. Behavioral objectivists warn us of the dangers in confusing the strategy, the means of achieving the objective, with the end, the objective itself. What they have failed to recognize is that they have confused the indicator, the means of determining whether the objective has been achieved, with the true objective.
>
> Behavioral objectives contain both a goal component and a measurement component, but the goal component is too often deemphasized to the point that it is virtually non-existent. The behavioral objective becomes in fact a statement of a measurement to be taken sometime prior to the completion of the learning and program, under specified conditions, and with criteria for evaluation. Most so-called behavioral objectives are not really objectives, therefore. They are only indicators (samples of behavior or tests that serve as evidence) that the true objectives have been achieved. Calling them objectives can mislead the teacher and the student into believing that the sample of behavior (the indicator), from which it is inferred that learning has taken place, is the desired end result of the learning activity. We agree with Mager (1968, p. 11) that "learning is for the future," but

behavioral objectives can easily result in a focus on the requirements of the present....

Behavioral objectives too often have not resulted in better objectives as much as [sometimes] in better measurement. But the measurement is not always clearly related to a meaningful future goal. With the focus on the indicators, it is easy to lose sight of the true objectives. Providing the student with a comprehensive set of behavioral objectives amounts to explaining in some detail the kinds of examinations he will be given. The indicators help him understand what he must do to satisfy the teacher or meet the requirements of the system, but unless special effort is made to relate the indicator (behavioral objective) to the true objective, performing the prescribed act or demonstrating the behavior may have little meaning for the student.

This gap between the indicator and the objective can only be overcome by special effort to achieve transfer. This effort would not be required, however, if objectives were written that had meaning in the personal life of the student beyond the classroom. Such objectives would have to include something other than a statement of a test performance.

(Wight, 1972)

As Wight implies, but does not state explicitly, there may be some very important objectives that are not readily amenable to testing. But if the objectives are important they should not be abandoned merely because they cannot be measured. Perhaps an objective of music education that is of considerable importance though not stated in behavioral terms and not readily measurable is to foster the enjoyment of music. Even behavioral indicators such as attendance at concerts, or verbal expressions of enjoyment, may not always be valid; going to concerts may be a response to social pressures of some kind, and the enthusiasm may be feigned, for the same reason.

As a matter of fact, though some objectives may seem impossible to measure, this may merely mean that thus far nobody has thought of a way to do it with a paper-and-pencil objective test. But someone may come along tomorrow and think of a way. That would not change the importance of the objective; it would only change the accuracy with which attainment of the objective can be assessed.

If some objectives are retained that the criterion-referenced test does not cover, there should be an explicit statement to this effect. (The same thing applies to norm-referenced tests, incidentally.)

Thus, insofar as is possible the educational objectives should determine the tests, but *the tests should never determine the objectives.*

The worst manifestation of the situation in which a test determines the objectives occurs when the objectives on which the teacher concentrates are not the objectives as stated, but the small sample represented by the items of the test. This is what is called "teaching to the test," and precautions should be taken against it if education is to be meaningful. It should be noted in this connection that the teaching-to-the-test problem is not a monopoly of criterion-referenced tests. It is also a problem with norm-referenced tests.

It is clear that objectives that are determined by the test are unlikely to be "valid" objectives. However it must be recognized that formal "validation of objectives" is seldom if ever possible, since basically the determination of objectives involves (and *should* involve) value judgments.

Whenever the question of validation arises it calls for an answer to the question, "Validation for what?" Presumably the education of children has purposes beyond getting them to a point where they can pass next week's test. This brings us to the important distinction between immediate and ultimate objectives. Lindquist made this distinction clear a quarter of a century ago; it is unfortunate that some of the current advocates of behavioral objectives as a panacea overlook it. Lindquist said:

> Many of the basic objectives of school instruction cannot possibly be fully realized until long after the instruction has been concluded. For guidance in specific courses of instruction, however, it is common practice to set up less remote objectives—objectives which are capable of immediate attainment. Ideally, these immediate objectives should in every instance have been clearly and logically derived from accepted ultimate objectives, in full consideration of all relevant characteristics of the pupils who are to receive the instruction. Ideally, also, the immediate objectives should be supported by dependable empirical evidence that their attainment will eventually lead to or make possible the realization of the ultimate objectives. Finally,

the content and methods of instruction should, ideally, be logically selected, devised, and used with specific reference to these immediate and ultimate objectives, and should likewise be supported by convincing experimental evidence of their validity.

Unfortunately, this ideal relationship among ultimate objectives, immediate objectives, and the content and methods of instruction has only rarely been approximated in actual practice. Some of the content of current instruction, if derived at all from sound and accepted ultimate objectives, has been derived from them by a process of faulty inference, and contributes much less to the realization of the objectives than other content which could be substituted for it. . . .

For any subject in the school curriculum, particularly for the long-established subjects, many of the immediate objectives claimed for them have a similar origin. Indeed, one of the most common of all *real* objectives in teaching, in general, is "to teach the facts contained in the textbook." [Stated] objectives are often only another way of saying, "to know what is in the text." The really functional objectives of many school subjects—the day-by-day objectives that most teachers are actually trying to attain—are, in large part, *content* objectives of this type. . . .

The situation [is[of particularly serious concern with reference to educational achievement testing. . . .

There is nothing objectionable about content objectives, as such, in instruction, so long as the content is used in a manner appropriate to the outcomes ultimately sought, and so long as its proper relation to the ultimate objectives is recognized and understood.

(Lindquist, 1951, pp. 121–127)[2]

Though when Lindquist wrote that, it was before the era of criterion-referenced tests, everything he said applies to most of today's criterion-referenced testing.

In connection with the matter of ultimate objectives, insofar as any effort is made to consider them, it may be that they are often viewed too narrowly. "Ultimate objectives" can reasonably be regarded as objectives relevant to the lives of the children when they grow up and become adults. In view of this, the tremendous mobility of Americans must be considered. Perhaps when school administrators consider the children's eventual needs to be synonymous with what their needs will be if they live all their lives in the same community, they forget that this may not be the case.

Children who are educated in a school system where the prevalent philosophy is, "Everyone in this town works in the [fill in name] plant, so that is what we should prepare the kids for," those kids may be getting shortchanged in their education. By the time they are 25 years old some of them may be living a couple of thousand miles from where they grew up. Thus, if the immediate "behavioral objectives" are too narrow, sometimes the ultimate objectives may have the same fault.

Although some of the statements made in this section may have given readers of this book the idea that the author is opposed to the use of "behavioral objectives," that is certainly not true. But it *is* necessary to be aware of their limitations so as not to regard them uncritically and use them unwisely.

Readers who wish to know more about the viewpoint of those who are more firmly committed to the concept of behavioral objectives as the essential framework for education than the author of this book is are urged to read some of the prolific writings of Mager (e.g. 1962), Popham and Baker (e.g. 1970), and Popham (e.g. 1974).

TEST RATIONALES

The test rationale (Flanagan, 1951a)[3] is the link between what behaviors are to be measured (i.e. the domain or the objectives, expressed as behaviors) and how they are to be measured (i.e. the test items). One of the principal weaknesses of many tests that claim to be criterion-referenced is lack of attention to this linkage.

The rationale for a criterion-referenced test should contain at least four components:

   1. Detailed definition of what behaviors are to be measured. This consists essentially of domain definition or objectives definition as discussed in the previous section.
   2. Specifications for drawing from the domain or the universe of objectives a *sample* of behaviors that are to form the basis for the test items to be written. The procedure for sampling domain elements (word meanings) for the previously mentioned domain-referenced test to measure size of vocabulary is discussed in some detail in the

next section. This provides an example of how the matter can be handled in a situation where it happens to be a fairly complicated problem.

3. An analytic discussion of what is to be measured and how it is to be measured—including inferences as to what kinds of test items will provide the desired sorts of measures, and why. This is the all-important linkage between objective and test item, and providing it is probably the most difficult step in rationale-writing. It requires insight, ingenuity, inference, and sometimes a big inductive leap, to get from the objective the achievement of which is to be evaluated via test items, to the test items that are to provide this evaluation (or, to express it somewhat more precisely, to provide a basis for estimating the degree to which the objective has been achieved).

4. Detailed test specifications, including not only the number of items and general item format, but also specification as to the number of options per item if multiple choice, the desired distribution of item difficulties for specified groups, specification as to whether the test is to be highly speeded, slightly speeded, or a pure power test, etc. Sample items, accompanied by specific suggestions as to what kinds of items to write, are also an integral part of the test rationale. This particular aspect is discussed in more detail in the section "Writing the Test Items."

SAMPLING FROM THE DOMAIN

It should be noted that of the four components of a test rationale listed in the section above, the first, third, and fourth are identical for criterion-referenced tests and tests that are not criterion-referenced. Only the second component, sampling from the domain, may differ substantially. As a matter of fact this component may not be formally described in the rationale for a test that is not criterion-referenced since *formal* sampling from a domain is rare for such a test, (though almost always necessary for a domain-referenced test, and sometimes for an objective-referenced test).

If more than one form of a test is to be developed, it is absolutely essential that each new form be based on a new and independently drawn sampling of the content from the domain rather than just consisting of new items constructed to be parallel, item by item, to those in the initial form—or worse yet, merely changing a few words in each item.

In the case of the domain-referenced vocabulary test we have been using as an example, the definition and delineation of the entire domain (or universe) were discussed in the first section of this chapter. After this domain definition is completed, the next technical problems are concerned with how to select a sample that would represent it adequately. The primary problems here are how many words to sample, whether to have a stratified sample (i.e. whether to divide the domain into categories on some basis, and draw a separate subsample from each category), and how to draw the sample.

1. In connection with the first problem, it is obvious that the number of words in the sample has to be far larger than would be required for the usual vocabulary test, for two reasons (although practical considerations, primarily limitations in the amount of testing time available, put rather severe restrictions on the number of words it is feasible to include). In the first place, the domain-referenced test will of necessity include a substantial proportion of items so hard as to be almost wholly nonfunctioning, and also some items so *easy* that they will have the same limitation. Secondly, the number of items required to assign an *absolute* meaning to a person's score, with a specified degree of reliability, is considerably greater than the number required merely to assign *relative* meaning to his score (in other words to locate accurately his relative position within the group).

2. It was decided to use a stratified sampling procedure. The reasons for stratification and the conditions under which it is advantageous are discussed later in this section. The five strata are scales A–E, shown in Table 3-1. Also shown in this table is the number of items decided upon for each stratum,[4] the numbers of word meanings from which the samples were to be drawn, and the formulas to be used to calculate five estimates of vocabulary size (represented by the letters S, T, U, V, W).

3. The third problem in connection with deciding the specific word meanings on which to base test items concerned the mechanics of sampling the dictionary—more specifically the question of space sampling versus entry sampling.[5] We settled on selecting pages at regular intervals and then doing entry sampling on each selected page. Entry sampling is preferable to space sampling because the

latter produces bias in favor of easy words (E. L. Thorndike, 1924; Lorge and Chall, 1963). The procedure for selecting the sample of word meanings was as follows. After it had been decided how many test items to use for each stratum (n_i' = number of items for stratum i), n_i' pages equally spaced throughout the appropriate dictionary listing were selected. Starting from the top of each of these pages the k_i^{th} acceptable word meaning encountered (i.e. the k_i^{th} meaning not falling in any of the 17 excluded categories) was selected for the sample. The ordinal number k_i was constant for the entire stratum. If there were fewer than k_i acceptable word meanings on a selected page, counting was continued on subsequent pages until an acceptable meaning was encountered. The value k_i was chosen to be sufficiently high that it would not be likely to be a meaning for the first word entered on the page (i.e. the first lexical entry on the page). This precaution was taken because it seemed likely that since the initial lexical entry on each page was also printed conspicuously in the upper margin (as an aid to page location), in an attention-getting position, persons who use the dictionary frequently and acquire vocabulary readily may be somewhat more likely to be familiar with these words than with words in less conspicuous locations.

A second advantage of choosing k_i to be a number other than 1 was that it avoided the bias in favor of easy words that space sampling produces. (When k_i equals 1, the result amounts to a kind of space sampling.)

To give the reader some idea of the flavor of the word meanings in the five strata, Exhibit 3-1 shows ten representative word meanings from each of these strata. These ten-unit samples were selected in the same way as the ones actually used for the test.

Dividing the universe to be sampled from into strata that are more homogeneous (with respect to variables to be studied) makes the sample more representative and thus reduces sampling errors. No harm is done, usually, if the basis of stratification (e.g. the stratification variable) turns out to be unrelated to the variables on which greater homogeneity is desired, but neither does any benefit result. Therefore stratification is most likely to improve the sampling if the universe from which the sample is to be drawn is not truly homogeneous. A look at Exhibit 3-1 suggests that in the case of the vocabulary test, the stratification was beneficial. Stratum 1 clearly has more fairly easy words than any of the others.

Table 3-1. Stratified Sampling of the Content Domain, for Domain-referenced Vocabulary Test (Form B).

Scale A-E	Stratum		No. of items[a]	Approx. no. of word meanings in population (i.e. stratum)	Item Weight (= no. of word meanings represented by each test item.)[a]
A	Stratum 1	Words in Merriam-Webster *Pocket Dictionary* (small paperback dictionary).	198[b]	39,251	198
B	Stratum 2	Words in the Merriam-Webster *New Collegiate Dictionary* that are not in the Merriam-Webster *Pocket Dictionary*.	72	56,149	780
C	Stratum 3	Words in the main body of the Merriam-Webster unabridged dictionary (2nd edition) that are not in the *New Collegiate Dictionary*.	88	127,709	1,451
D	Stratum 4	Words in the entries at the bottom of the page in the Merriam-Webster unabridged dictionary (2nd edition). (None of these words is in the *New Collegiate Dictionary*.)	36	41,794	1,161
E	Stratum 5	Words in the Addenda (the new words section) in the Merriam-Webster unabridged dictionary (2nd edition) that are not in the *New Collegiate Dictionary*.	6	1,365	228
		TOTAL	400		

S-W Composite Scores Derivable from Test

S = Estimated no. of word meanings known in stratum 1
T = Estimated no. of word meanings known in strata 1 + 2
U = Estimated no. of word meanings known in strata 1 + 2 + 3

V = Estimated no. of word meanings known in strata 1 + 2 + 3 + 4
W = Estimated no. of word meanings known in strata 1 + 2 + 3 + 4 + 5

S = Estimated no. of word meanings known in pocket dictionary
T = Estimated no. of word meanings known in collegiate dictionary
U = Estimated no. of word meanings known in unabridged dictionary, main listing[d]
V = Estimated no. of word meanings known in unabridged dictionary, main listing plus bottom-of-page listing[d]
W = Estimated no. of word meanings known in unabridged dictionary

[a] The numbers of items, and accordingly the weights, shown here for "Form B" of the test differ somewhat from those used in the test actually constructed in 1960 (Form A). The Form B characteristics represent our current judgment as to the better way to proceed.
[b] 197 items printed and scored; one item (for an *extremely* easy word) is not printed in the test but is assumed correct for all examinees.
[c] Formulas for estimates of vocabulary size

$$S = 198 + 198A$$
$$T = 198 + 198A + 780B$$
$$U = 198 + 198A + 780B + 1451C$$
$$V = 198 + 198A + 780B + 1451C + 1161D$$
$$W = 198 + 198A + 780B + 1451C + 1161D + 228E$$

In these formulas above, A–E are the raw scores (corrected for chance) on strata 1–5 respectively. (A is based on 197 items.)
In the formulas for S, T, U, V, and W, shown above, the values used for A, B, C, D, and E are K' test scores. These are scores corrected by the usual formula for correction for chance, with negative scores changed to 0.
[d] Plus word meanings in New Words Addenda that are also in collegiate dictionary.

Exhibit 3-1. Examples[a] of Word Meanings in Each Stratum of Domain-referenced Vocabulary Test.

Stratum 1

1. alien (*n.*)
2. cassava
3. dilapidation
4. gape (*n.*, *#1*, yawn)
5. latticework
6. outright
7. reciprocity (*n.*, *#1*, cooperation)
8. span (*n.*, *#2*, spread between supports)
9. touching (*adj.*, pathetic)
10. viridescent

Stratum 2

1. belemnite
2. contagium
3. equalitarian (*n.*)
4. haul (*v.i.*)
5. leaf (*v.t.*, to leaf a book)
6. nunciature
7. prophylaxis
8. shandygaff
9. terete
10. whites (*n.pl.*, *med.*)

Stratum 3

1. aristogenesis
2. chamoisite
3. discovery (*n.*, *mining*)
4. generalia
5. juck
6. nephradenoma
7. pray (*v.i.*, please)
8. scissorbill
9. sure (*adj.*, *#8*, as in "to be sure")
10. veruled

Stratum 4

1. aromatous
2. chapterful
3. dislodgeable
4. geoffroyine
5. jurisdictionalism
6. neurohypnology
7. preclothe
8. Scorpiones
9. suspectable
10. vice-admiralship

Stratum 5

1. agape (*n.*, brotherly love)
2. bobeche
3. court (*n.*, motel)
4. faciation
5. historicism
6. make (*n.*, shuffle of cards)
7. palynology
8. quadrivalent (*adj.*, *genetics*)
9. sniperscope
10. track (*n.*, *aeronautics*)

[a]None of the word meanings shown here was in the sample actually used for the test.

NOTE: For multimeaning words, the part of speech is indicated in parentheses and if this does not delimit the word meaning adequately, the specific meaning is also indicated briefly.

In this discussion of sampling, thus far we have concentrated on a domain-referenced test as an example. The problems are a little less complex, perhaps, but more dangerous, in the case of objective-referenced tests. It is important to make certain that the universe from which the sampling is done covers the full range of the objective. Consider, for instance, the behavioral objective quoted above, "To be able to solve quadratic equations that have integral coefficients." Notice that there are no restrictions imposed on the size of the coefficients. That seems quite reasonable for an objective. Since the procedure (i.e. the formula) is the same regardless of the size of the coefficients, presumably it would be reasonable to expect any examinee who had learned how to solve quadratic equations to find the value of x in the following equation:

$$375,296x^2 - 491x = 52,448$$

Except for the much greater likelihood of computational errors (the avoidance of which, presumably, is not what the behavioral objective is primarily about), the above quadratic equation should be no more difficult to solve than this one:

$$3x^2 - 2x = 4$$

But the second equation would clearly be far more suitable for inclusion in an objective-referenced test for the quadratic-equation objective than would the first. The objections to inclusion of the first equation are manifold. Not only would the desired results (information as to whether the examinee has learned how to solve quadratic equations with integral coefficients) be badly contaminated by careless computation errors, it would also be intolerably time-consuming. Furthermore, drawing a true probability sample of integral coefficients within the not very restrictive range $-\infty$ to $+\infty$ would necessitate grossly unequal probabilities for different coefficients with consequent major disadvantages,[6] and no compensating advantages.

Of course it would be possible (and reasonable) to restrict the coefficients to the $+12$ to -12 range, or to the $+10$ to -10 range, or to the $+3$ to -3 range, or to any other such range that might seem convenient. But whatever range one selected would be arbitrary, and therefore selecting coefficients within it by a formal random sampling procedure would be quite pointless; impressive, perhaps, and scientific-appearing, but pointless nevertheless.

Let us generalize: Not only for the hypothetical objective discussed above but for most other instructional objectives as well, the emphasis that some writers have placed on the importance of formal random sampling from the domain of potential test items representing the objective seems excessive. There is nothing *wrong* with formal sampling when it happens to be more convenient to operate on that basis than not to (as, for instance, if one is using computer methodology to develop the test, or if a large number of parallel forms are being developed at the same time). But if formal random sampling is inconvenient, it should be reassuring to the conscientious test developer to know that he will probably end up with just as good a test if he does not bother about this nicety—perhaps even a better test, as a matter of fact, if he substitutes thought for the mindlessness of a random operation.

Whether or not the coefficients for the quadratic-equation items are selected randomly, it will be necessary to insure that all the types of solutions represented by the objective in the first form in which it is stated on page 23 are included in appropriate proportions. (Simple random selection does not insure this, particularly if the number of items is relatively small; therefore if a random procedure is being used it probably should be some sort of *stratified* random sample, for which quadratic equations with each type of solution constitute a separate stratum.) Should each type of solution then be treated as a separate subobjective? For instance should all the items for which both solutions are positive integers be isolated in a separate subtest? Certainly not; at least not if one is really concerned about whether the examinee can meet the objective of being able to solve quadratic equations. The objective does not say anything about having hints as to the nature of the solution. Isolating items in separate tests or separate subsections would provide such a hint, so the test would not be measuring the objective as stated.

Of course the fact that formal sampling from the domain of items for an objective-referenced test may not be necessary does not confer freedom to jockey the item content to give the kind of score distribution one hopes for. It is still necessary to have a clear concept of what the objectives are, and what the corresponding

Developing criterion-referenced tests

hypothetical domain of items is like, and to make an honest effort to get a reasonable representation of that domain. Let us suppose, for instance, that you have a ten-item criterion-referenced mathematics test for grade 8. Let us suppose further that this test has a very low success rate. Now suppose you are unhappy with the low success rate. All you have to do is add a large number of ridiculously easy items that virtually everyone will get right. For instance you might use items something like the following:

> The number forty-six is
> A. 8
> B. 19
> C. 32
> D. 46
> E. 77

It is easy to see that if you add 50 items like that to the test, it will add about 50 points to everyone's score and to the mean, giving something closer to the kind of distribution hoped for, but considerably further away from the kind of test needed. This is not a legitimate ploy.

WRITING THE TEST ITEMS

After the procedure for determining the sample of domain elements on which test items are to be written has been determined, it is necessary to tackle the problem of how to measure mastery of these word meanings. The fact that this problem is postponed until all of the other ones—about definition of the domain and selection of the sample of domain elements—are settled does not minimize its importance. As has already been indicated a discussion of what kinds of test items are to be written is an integral part of the test rationale, and it involves decisions at several levels. For instance, in the case of the domain-referenced test of vocabulary that has been used as an example throughout this chapter, some of the problems with which it was necessary to deal in the rationale, and the manner of dealing with them, have already been discussed under "Defining the Domain." For example, as was indicated in that section, it was decided that the test would be designed to measure recognition, not recall, and that it would be concerned with general comprehension of the printed word, but not with subtleties and very fine distinctions. But how are items to be written that will achieve these ends? The test rationale of course contained a very full discussion of this matter, starting with item type and then going into an exhaustive discussion of what kind of items to write and what kind to avoid, within the restrictions of the chosen type.

Item type

The idea of using open-end questions, where the examinee would be asked to supply definitions, was considered carefully and rejected flatly, as introducing more problems than it would solve. The item type decided upon was the five-option multiple-choice item.

One of the advantages that is sometimes attributed to items of the constructed-answer type, as opposed to multiple-choice items, is that the former type essentially eliminates guessing as a factor. But as pointed out by Davis and Diamond (1974) this is not necessarily true. For a great many areas, a *well-constructed* multiple-choice test will prove generally superior to a test of the constructed-answer type, even a well-constructed one. The multiple-choice test is clearly superior in ease of scoring, and usually in objectivity of scoring as well; also in reliability. And if it is well constructed it is at least equal to the constructed-answer test in relevance and validity.

Item writing

How to construct multiple-choice items (for the domain-referenced vocabulary test) that would yield scores to which reasonably accurate *absolute* meaning could be assigned, instead of just relative meaning, was perhaps the most difficult technical problem in the entire venture.

To increase the likelihood that if an examinee answered an item incorrectly it was because he did not understand the word meaning being tested, rather than because he failed to understand other words in the item, an effort was made, insofar as possible, to couch all items in terms simpler than the word meaning being tested.

Occasionally this was impossible. For instance, one word, "about," used as a preposition with the meaning "concerning," was so resistant to efforts along this line that we decided more accurate results would be obtained by just *assuming* that any high school student would know this word and adding the appropriate constant to their scores to allow for it. It is worth noting, in this connection, that it is the very *easy* words, not the very *hard* ones, for which it is difficult to write good test items.

As for level of difficulty and specificity of the items, Exhibit 3-2 may throw some light on how this problem was approached in constructing the test. This exhibit shows several items that might be written to test understanding of the word "icosahedron," and corresponding items to test "octahedron." The items are arranged in order of specificity, number 1 being easiest and most general, and number 3 items being most specific.

If "icosahedron" had been one of the words in the sample, we probably would have used item 3a. Item 1 is too vague. Does a person really *know* what an icosahedron is if he merely knows that it has something to do with geometry, or worse still, if he does not know that much but is able to eliminate options because he happens to be a ballet addict, a biology expert, or a tropical fish buff?

Now let us consider items 2 and 3b in Exhibit 3-2. Should we give someone credit for knowing what an icosahedron is merely because he knows what a polyhedron is? Probably not. "Polyhedron" is a far easier (i.e. more common) word than "icosahedron," and we do not want to make it look as if more people understand "icosahedron" than really do.

If one knows what a polyhedron is (i.e. a certain kind of geometrical solid) and infers that an icosahedron is a kind of polyhedron (a reasonable inference), one has the answer to item 2, and with just a little more knowledge about polyhedrons one also can answer item 3b. But one still does not really know what an icosahedron is unless he knows it is a polyhedron *with 20 faces,* just as an octahedron is a polyhedron *with 8 faces.* The number of faces an octahedron has can be inferred easily by someone with only a rudimentary knowledge of Greek or Latin roots; the same is not true of an icosahedron. Ideally the item should test knowledge of the whole word—not merely the easiest part of the word. But if it is not convenient to

Exhibit 3-2. Construction of Domain-referenced Vocabulary Test: Selecting the Degree of Specificity of Knowledge to Be Tested.

Icosahedron

1. An icosahedron is a kind of

    A. tropical fish.
    B. bat.
    C. moth.
    D. ballet step.
    *E. geometrical figure.

2. An icosahedron is a kind of

    A. polyhedral angle.
    B. two-dimensional geometrical figure.
    *C. geometrical solid.
    D. curve in three-dimensional space.
    E. hypothetical four-dimensional figure.

Octahedron

1. An octahedron is a kind of

    A. tropical fish.
    B. bat.
    C. moth.
    D. ballet step.
    *E. geometrical figure.

2. An octahedron is a kind of

    A. polyhedral angle.
    B. two-dimensional geometrical figure.
    *C. geometrical solid.
    D. curve in three-dimensional space.
    E. hypothetical four-dimensional figure.

3a. An icosahedron is a polyhedron with

　　A. 11 faces.
　　B. 12 faces.
　　C. 15 faces.
　*D. 20 faces.
　　E. 50 faces.

3b. An icosahedron is a geometrical solid with 20

　　A. vertices.
　　B. edges.
　*C. faces.
　　D. edges at each vertex.
　　E. sides per face.

3a. An octahedron is a polyhedron with

　　A. 4 faces.
　　B. 6 faces.
　*C. 8 faces.
　　D. 12 faces.
　　E. 16 faces.

3b. An octahedron is a geometrical solid with 8

　　A. vertices.
　　B. edges.
　*C. faces.
　　D. edges at each vertex.
　　E. sides per face.

NOTE: The items considered most suitable for inclusion in a domain-referenced vocabulary test are enclosed in boxes.

cover the whole word in the options, the harder part of the word should be tested—i.e. "icosa" rather than "hedron"—on the assumption that if one knows the harder part he is likely to know the easier part.

By the same logic, item 2 (or perhaps 3b) would be preferable to item 3a if the word "octahedron" had been selected for the sample instead of "icosahedron," since the prefix "octa" is easier than the suffix "hedron," and the item should therefore stress understanding of the latter.

Principles such as this were used throughout the test wherever appropriate, in constructing the items.

It is worth noting at this point that some of the vocabulary tests that have been developed in the past have suffered from a too slavish dependence on verbatim use of sometimes complex, oblique, or otherwise difficult dictionary definitions. As a result an examinee who really had an adequate understanding of the word being tested might still not be able to answer the item correctly. Other vocabulary tests have been equally handicapped, though in a somewhat different way, by slavish dependence on thesaurus categories. In developing the domain-referenced vocabulary test, a concerted effort was made not to fall into these traps. Thus in order to test understanding of a specific word meaning it is sometimes desirable to depart from the usual vocabulary item by reversing stem and options—in other words by using the word itself as the key answer and the desired definition in the stem, instead of vice versa. This device is particularly useful in the case of multimeaning words, where one of the less common meanings is the one being tested. Consider, for instance, "possessions" as a definition of "effects." To test knowledge of that particular meaning, the following would be a very poor item:

"Effects" means
   A. positions.
 *B. possessions.
   C. beliefs.
   D. causes.
   E. trials.

The trouble with this item is that the stem does not provide an adequate "set" for the examinee concerning the particular meaning of "effects" that is intended. The following item, in which the word "effects" becomes the key answer, would be preferable:

> A person's possessions are sometimes called his
> A. results.
> B. consequences.
> C. actions.
> D. causes.
> *E. effects.

By far the simplest and most direct way of testing understanding of word meanings turns out in many instances to be through the use of examples rather than definitions. For instance suppose the word "rhyme" with the intransitive verb meaning "to accord in rhyme; to form a rhyme" had been selected. Consider how much simpler the following item is than one that uses a formal definition would be.

> Which of the following pairs of words rhyme?
> A. continue, contain.
> *B. notion, ocean.
> C. table, noble.
> D. fiddle, dribble.
> E. here, hear.

Diagrams constitute another device that helps to simplify some items so that examinees understanding the word meaning being tested will be almost certain to select the right answer. Exhibit 3-3 shows three items aimed at testing understanding of a particular adjectival definition of "spiral." Each item represents a different approach and each has one and only one correct answer. But in the writer's opinion these items range from atrocious to effective. Item 1 clearly belongs in the former category, for many reasons; not the least of these is the fault alluded to earlier, slavish dependence on verbatim use of dictionary definitions. Item 2 suffers from this same defect and is only a little better than item 1. What little improvement there is derives from the greater brevity resulting from transfer of the definition to the stem. The particular meaning of "spiral" being tested is one that seems to call for the use of diagrams in the item, in order to achieve the requisite simplicity. Anyone who really understands the word "spiral" when it is used in the sense of the particular definition under consideration should have no difficulty whatever with item 3. The person who knows

Exhibit 3-3. Construction of Domain-referenced Vocabulary Test: Illustrating the Appropriate Use of Diagrams, and the Inappropriate Use of Dictionary Definitions.

Below are three items to test knowledge of the following adjectival definition of "spiral":

> "Winding, coiling, or circling round a center or pole and gradually receding from (or approaching) it."

The items are judged to be arranged in ascending order of effectiveness.

Item 1. "Spiral" means:

    A. traveling in an elliptical orbit.

    B. circling round a center or pole at a uniform distance from it and constantly within a single plane.

  *C. winding, coiling, or circling round a center or pole and gradually receding from (or approaching) it.

    D. consisting of a finite set of concentric spheres at uniform distances apart.

    E. consisting of an infinite set of concentric coplanar circles whose radii constitute a geometric series.

Item 2. A path that winds, coils, or circles round a center or pole and gradually recedes from (or approaches) it is said to be:

    A. spherical.
    B. circular.
    C. concentric.
  *D. spiral.
    E. parabolic.

Item 3. Which of these shapes is spiral?

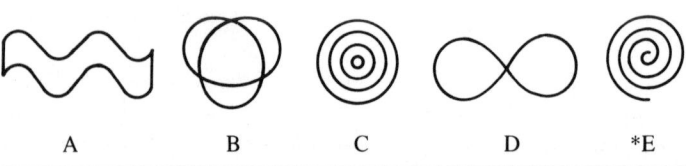

  A   B   C   D   *E

perfectly well what a spiral is and can visualize it, but who when asked to define it can only say something like, "You know; it's like this," while moving his index finger in a spiral would be able to answer item 3 correctly; he might have considerable difficulty with items 1 and 2 in Exhibit 3-3.

Still another procedure used occasionally to produce simpler, clearer items is to make a slight change in the form of the word to be tested. For instance a noun might be changed from singular to plural (provided its plural were not an irregular form). Or perhaps a verb (e.g. "consider") might be put in participial form (e.g. "was considering" or "has considered"). However no *radical* changes may be made in the form of the word since any change necessitates the assumption that everyone understanding one version of the word would also understand the other version.

Exhibit 3-4 is a verbatim but considerably abridged extract from the item-type specifications that were incorporated in the rationale for the domain-referenced vocabulary test.

Throughout this chapter we have returned repeatedly to a discussion of how the construction of a criterion-referenced test was handled in the case of a particular vocabulary test constructed a decade and a half ago. The reader may wonder why. It is certainly not because we are under the impression that most of the readers of this book will need to construct domain-referenced vocabulary tests. Rather, our intent is to illustrate the nature and complexity of the problems that arise in constructing a criterion-referenced test (the vocabulary test seemed to provide illustrations of almost all these problems) and to show how it is possible to cope with these problems if one thinks them through carefully and considers the implications of various possible solutions before adopting any.

But it has also been our intent to show that constructing a good test is not an easy matter—and that a criterion-referenced test may sometimes be even more difficult to construct than a test that is not criterion-referenced. Our purpose in this is not to discourage test construction efforts but rather to urge that where feasible, administrators arrange to have tests that are to be widely used written by experienced and expert test writers, rather than delegating the job to minimally trained clerks. Or at the very least, if it is necessary to

Exhibit 3-4. Extracts from Rationale for Domain-referenced Vocabulary Test (Abridged Extracts from Item-type Specifications and from Instructions for Item Writers).

Many of the items will be of the following type:

1. "Questionable" means

   A. inquiring.
   *B. doubtful.
   C. inquisitive.
   D. true.
   E. false.

2. "Magnitude" means

   A. generosity.
   *B. size.
   C. location.
   D. kindness.
   E. direction.

Some items may be of a somewhat different type from the synonym type shown above. For instance:

3. A nocturnal animal is one that sleeps

   A. all winter.
   B. upside-down.
   *C. in the daytime.
   D. in a tree.
   E. underground.

items, which test understanding of the words "nocturnal," "amphibian," "novelist," and "federal" respectively, is the stem of the form "_____ means."

In view of the fact that because the proposed vocabulary test is based on a probability sample of word meanings, the item writer does not have the usual option of throwing out any words that prove unusually difficult to write items around, he will have to resort to whatever expedients may be necessary in order to develop a multiple-choice item which tests whether the examinee is familiar with and understands the sampled word. One expedient that may be necessary in the case of a small number of items might be the use of diagrams or pictures. For instance to test familiarity with the word "birdhouse" the following item might be used:

7. The thing shown in the picture is usually called

   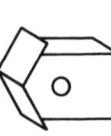

   A. a bird apartment.
   B. an artificial bird nest.
   *C. a birdhouse.
   D. a bird home.
   E. a bird building.

Understanding of the meaning of "three" can be tested quite simply by the following item:

9. "Three" is the number between

   *A. two and four.
   B. four and six.
   C. six and eight.
   D. seven and nine.
   E. eight and ten.

It is quite true that to answer this question correctly the examinee must have the concept not only of "three" but also of "two" and "four," and "between." However the probability that he will know what "three" means and will not know what "two" and "four" mean, or will not be able to infer the meaning of "between" from context if he does not know the word, is too slight to warrant concern. The only examinees who conceivably would have difficulty with this item would be illiterates and those whose native language is not English and who have not yet mastered the language. But in view of the purpose of the test it is conceivable that it could be used for examinees whose knowledge of English is borderline. However understanding of the word "three" might be tested more directly by item 10 or 11.

4. Which of these is an amphibian?

   A. Dog.
   B. Bird.
   C. Camel.
   *D. Frog.
   E. Worm.

5. A novelist writes

   A. poetry.
   *B. fiction.
   C. biography.
   D. history books.
   E. songs.

6. The government of the United States is called "federal" because it has

   A. a president.
   B. three separate branches.
   C. free elections.
   *D. separate states.
   E. separation of Church and State.

It should be noted that in none of these four

This expedient would avoid the necessity of having the stem "A birdhouse is a" followed by the excessively obviously key answer "house for birds," or even of having the stem "A birdhouse is a man-made shelter for" followed by the key answer "birds."

However wherever it is possible to develop satisfactory items without the use of pictures this should be done. For "birdhouse," for instance, the following item may be somewhat preferable to the picture item above:

8. A man-made shelter for wild birds is usually called

   A. a bird apartment.
   B. an artificial bird nest.
   *C. a birdhouse.
   D. a bird home.
   E. a bird building.

10. How many stars?
        * * *

    A. Six.
    B. Four.
    C. Nine.
    *D. Three.
    E. Two.

11. Which row has *three* stars?

    A. * * *
    *B. * * * * *
    C. * * * * * *
    D. * * * * * * *
    E. * * * * * * * *

Note that in item 10, the options are deliberately arranged out of numerical order, so as not to give any clue to an examinee who really is not sure of the meaning of "three".

The following question might be used for the word "these".

12. "*These* things" means the things that are

    A. there.
    *B. here.
    C. nowhere.
    D. everywhere.
    E. anywhere.

The item writer should check each item carefully in the dictionary to make certain that none of the distractors might be considered a defensible answer on the basis of some obscure secondary meaning of the word.

have the bulk of the item writing done by clerical personnel, their initial efforts should be viewed as training exercises, not finished products, and should be supervised by an experienced test writer. (None of this, of course, is intended to refer to teacher-made tests that are just to be used within the teacher's own classroom.)

Like almost any other type of writing, writing test items expertly is an art, not a science. Conceivably some day it will be a science; but it certainly is not one now. Efforts have been made to routinize it. (In fact, some supposedly simple tests, such as vocabulary tests, have been written by computer.) In our view, such efforts are interesting stunts, but at this stage they are little more.

We are also well aware, of course, of the efforts in recent years to reduce item writing to a clerical routine through the use of a standardized item format, consisting of an invariant part called an "item shell" or "item form," within which certain variables are to be replaced by members of specified replacement sets. Hively (1968, 1970) and Nitko (1970) are among the numerous researchers who have been active in developing this approach.

An example of an item shell for a vocabulary test might be:

"_____" means:
A. _____
B. _____
C. _____
D. _____
E. _____

where the blank in each item stem is to be filled in by one of the words selected in sampling from the dictionary, and the key answer is to be a verbatim quotation of the dictionary definition. In the case of multimeaning words the particular definition to be quoted would also be selected by random sampling. The distractors would also be determined objectively, in accordance with a set of predetermined rules. Such a procedure, however, would not lead to a good test. We have already pointed out, earlier in this chapter, the disadvantages resulting from restricting vocabulary item answers to verbatim quotation of dictionary definitions.

Computer-constructed tests (Richards, 1967) and tests based on the "item-shell" principle seem almost inevitably to have substantially lower reliability than tests of the same length in which the items have been individually and carefully constructed by expert test writers. (A reduction in reliability on the order of magnitude of a drop from over .90 to about .80 would be quite likely.) On this basis the increase in test reliability that can be achieved through construction by human experts rather than by a computer program is equivalent to more than doubling the length of the test. In general, tests constructed on the item-shell principle, even if constructed directly by human beings, are likely to have about the same level of reliability as computer-constructed tests. This is because the computer program is likely to incorporate essentially the same rules for item generation as are followed by humans generating items to fill item shells.

The only likely exception—in other words the only situation in which a test developed via item shells may come close in reliability to a test in which items and options are constructed individually and thoughtfully—is a test in which there is only one possible correct answer that might be provided for each item. A vocabulary test does not meet that criterion; any definition may be worded in more than one way. But a test of ability to add two two-digit numbers *does*. For instance consider an item shell of the following form:

$$\underline{} + \underline{} = \underline{}$$

If one of the items were:

$$46 + 17 = \underline{}$$

there is no key answer possible other than ''63.'' (But even in this situation a better test will result if the distractors are constructed by a test writer who knows what kinds of addition errors are likely than if random generation of numbers is used to create distractors, or if they are generated by arbitrary rules.)

Our conclusion that in general tests constructed by knowledgeable experts are substantially superior to those constructed by computer program or in accordance with arbitrary preestablished rules that leave no leeway for judgment is precisely in line with the statement by Davis and Diamond (1974) that ''differences in the psychological insight, conscientiousness, and experience of the item writer have greater effect on the quality and other characteristics of test items than other variables.''

TRYOUT AND ITEM ANALYSIS

For domain-referenced tests

The first question to ask in connection with tryout and item analysis of a criterion-referenced test is, "Are these steps necessary?"

In the case of a norm-referenced test it is customary to develop somewhat more items for the tryout form of the test than will be needed for the final form. Furthermore if a distribution of item content has been specified in advance for the final form of the test, a rather common procedure in the case of norm-referenced achievement tests, enough extra items are provided in each content area that it will be possible to meet content specifications for the final test even after items have been eliminated on the basis of item analysis results. None of this is precisely true for the typical domain-referenced test. Each item in such a test is likely to correspond to a domain element picked in the content sampling; in such a case none of the items can be eliminated. However, items *can* be eliminated if more than one item has been written explicitly for each item slot. For instance in the case of the domain-referenced vocabulary test discussed earlier in this chapter, if two entirely distinct items had been constructed for each word meaning selected for the sample, that would have been a situation in which item analysis would have been very useful, to select the more effective item. However that was not done; only one item was constructed for each word meaning sampled. Because of the very explicit item specifications in the test rationale, for most word meanings it would not have been possible to construct multiple items within the tight constraints imposed. The same thing would be true for many other domain-referenced tests. In the case of such tests the onus is on the item writers to an even greater extent than usual, to write good items, since the expedient of throwing out poor items is not available. Thus item analysis is not nearly as essential for some domain-referenced tests as it is for most norm-referenced ones. But even for domain-referenced tests that have to be constructed in such a way that items cannot be thrown out after tryout, item analysis may nevertheless prove useful (particularly if the item writers are relatively inexperienced) to identify items or options that seem not to be working well (in terms, primarily, of their coefficients of

Developing criterion-referenced tests 51

internal consistency,[7] which should be substantially positive for the key answer and negative for each distractor). In a domain-referenced test that does not include item-for-item parallel items poor items cannot be thrown out, but they *can* often be substantially improved—perhaps by revising some of the distractors.

For objective-referenced tests

In the case of an objective-referenced test consisting of a substantial number of items measuring a single objective, it is quite likely that all the items will have been constructed to be extremely homogeneous. If so, this will be apparent from inspection; for instance a test to measure ability to add pairs of two-digit numbers, where all the items are of the form "_____ + _____ = ?" (the blanks being replaced by two-digit numbers). For such a test, tryout and item analysis are entirely superfluous. The only helpful thing they might indicate is errors in the scoring key—and it should certainly be possible to locate those faster and more economically in some other way.

In any event if extra items *have* been written for a tryout form, with the expectation that some will be eliminated for the final form, it is crucial that the final test consist of items that conform exactly to the original plan for content distribution. It cannot be emphasized too strongly, however, that this is equally true for criterion-referenced tests and tests that are not criterion-referenced. In this book we have devoted considerable attention to pointing out numerous prevalent misconceptions about criterion-referenced tests. But here we come upon a misconception that applies primarily to norm-referenced tests; it impinges on criterion-referenced tests only in the sense that criterion-referenced tests are alleged to differ from norm-referenced tests in a way in which actually they do *not* differ. The misconception to which we are referring is really a multifaceted one; the litany goes something like this:

> Criterion-referenced tests are not at all like norm-referenced tests in terms of desirable item characteristics.
> When the final form of a norm-referenced test is being developed, items are selected for it solely on the basis of item statistics; no

attention is paid to content distribution. *This is not true of criterion-referenced tests.*

The ideal norm-referenced test would consist of items with difficulty coefficients (proportion of the group knowing the answer) as close to .50 as possible. *This is not true of criterion-referenced tests, which should ideally consist of items that everyone can answer correctly.*

In picking items for a norm-referenced test it is customary to select the items that have the highest coefficients of internal consistency— in other words the most discriminating items. *This is not true of criterion-referenced tests.*

Now let us examine this litany to see exactly what is wrong with it. In the first place items for the final form of a well-constructed norm-referenced achievement test are *not* selected solely on the basis of item statistics. Considerable attention is (or should be) paid to the distribution of item content, which should be an integral part of the specifications for the test.

In the second place an achievement test with all item difficulties at about the .50 level is far from ideal. To the extent that the test is measuring a single more-or-less homogeneous ability or field of knowledge, a wide range of item difficulty levels is desirable— perhaps from .10 to .90, or possibly even from .05 to .95 (with a mean close to the .50 level). The higher the intercorrelations among the items the wider the range of item difficulties that is desirable (in order to spread the scores appropriately). By the same token, the only sort of achievement test on which it is desirable to have all the item difficulties very close to the .50 level is one on which the items are essentially uncorrelated. But if the items *are* uncorrelated it is hard to understand why one would want to combine them to get a total "achievement score" since it would not represent achievement in any definable field.[8]

In the third place, in a well-constructed norm-referenced achievement test it is *not* customary to pick only the "most discriminating items" (i.e. the items with the highest coefficients of internal consistency).Doing that would virtually guarantee that the item content specifications would not be met. The subset of items selected would be those items most alike in terms of content, thus virtually eliminating the possibility of adequate content coverage. It

Developing criterion-referenced tests

is quite unlikely that a very good achievement test could be developed by limiting it only to the "most discriminating items" particularly if the number of items tried out happened to be two or three times as large as the number needed for the final form.

General considerations

How, then, should item analysis data be used to develop the final form of a norm-referenced test, and how should practices differ for a criterion-referenced test? The answer for a norm-referenced test is that the item analysis information only supplements content distribution considerations; it does not replace them. Items with negative, zero, or low positive coefficients of internal consistency for the key answers should be thrown out. If any of the distractors for an item that is retained has a positive coefficient of internal consistency, which would indicate that it is working in the wrong direction, that distractor should be revised, in such a way as not to invalidate the rest of the item. If a few other minor changes in options or in wording of the stem of otherwise satisfactory items seem desirable on the basis of item analysis results, the changes should be made, but they should be few in number. From the items that remain (all of which, presumably, have satisfactory coefficients of internal consistency) a set should be selected that has the right content distribution and approximates the desired distribution of item difficulty indexes. *Other things being equal,* preference should be given to those items with the highest coefficients of internal consistency—but such preference should never be given at the expense of a priori decisions on item content coverage and item difficulty distribution. So much for the uses of item analysis in constructing a norm-referenced test.

But what about a criterion-referenced test? The answer is that when an item analysis is carried out, the results will be used in almost the same way. The chief differences are as follows:

   1. For a criterion-referenced test, the content distribution specifications are much more rigid and more restrictive, because of the inherent nature of the criterion-referencing feature.

   2. The group on which the item analysis data are based is different. Instead of consisting of students who are homogeneous with

respect to amount of exposure to the course materials (e.g. all end-of-year testings, or all midyear testings) it should consist of two or more subgroups—those with no exposure to the materials (pretest situation), those who have completed or nearly completed the course or the unit (posttest situation), and possibly some who are somewhere in between.

3. Instead of coefficients of internal consistency, computed for each item against the total score, item validity coefficients should be computed against amount of exposure.

It cannot be emphasized too strongly that items should *not* be thrown out merely because they fail to show close to 100% correct in the posttest situation. There is no point in testing performance if results one is unhappy with are going to be ignored. If an item provides a bona fide measure of a stated objective and that objective is not being met, that is important information, which should not be concealed by discarding items that reveal the deficiency.

As a matter of fact if an item were truly one to which 100% of the examinees would know the answer, and if that were known in advance, there would be no point in wasting anyone's time administering and scoring that item. (Certainly anyone who does not know the letters of the alphabet cannot be expected to get through college but nobody seriously suggests that knowledge of the alphabet is among the things on which college applicants should be tested.)

NOTES

[1] The basic concept of the test was developed by John C. Flanagan, who is cited in Chapter 1 as one of the progenitors of the notion of criterion-referenced tests (though he did not use that term), and the test itself was developed by the author of this book, for use in Project TALENT.

[2] Readers interested in the problem of instructional objectives are urged to read the entire chapter by Lindquist from which this quotation was taken.

[3] Those who are involved in test planning and test writing are urged to read this article.

[4] The numbers of items shown in Table 3-1 for some of the strata differ somewhat from the numbers that were actually used in 1960 (and of course the weights differ accordingly). Table 3-1 represents our current judgment as to a reasonable distribution of items, representing a reasonable compromise between having items from all the strata equally weighted, to minimize sampling errors, and having heavier item weights for items from the easier strata, in order to reduce measurement errors.

Developing criterion-referenced tests

[5] By "space sampling" is meant sampling on the basis of position on the page (e.g. halfway down the first column). "Entry sampling" means actually counting the entries (word meanings in this case).

[6] For an extremely large coefficient, the probability of selection would have to be extremely small (approaching zero), and consequently any item involving such a coefficient would have to have an absurdly large weight, with a resulting grossly deleterious effect on test reliability.

[7] The coefficient of internal consistency may be defined as the biserial correlation between whether a particular option is selected and total score on the test.

[8] The probable source of misunderstanding on the part of those writers who believe that every item on a norm-referenced test should have a difficulty index as close to .50 as possible lies in the fact that they are confusing achievement tests (for which an external criterion is seldom either available or appropriate) with predictive tests or other tests for which an external criterion is available. For such tests, items with close-to-zero intercorrelations, but with substantial correlations with the external criterion, are desirable in order that an appropriately weighted combination of the items will predict the external criterion well. (For such a test, and for such a use, items whose difficulties cluster at the .50 level work well. But such tests are far from the conventional norm-referenced achievement test intended for use in schools.)

4
Norms

Norms? For a criterion-referenced test? Yes, norms for a criterion-referenced test!

NEED FOR NORMS

In Chapter 2 the question was asked, "Can a test be both criterion-referenced and norm-referenced at the same time?" The answer given was an unequivocal yes. We shall go even further now and say that for effective planning and effective use of a criterion-referenced test, norms are not merely possible—they are actually essential (at least in most situations and for most uses). How else would the user know what level of performance is reasonable to expect? Should a two-year-old child be expected to have a vocabulary of 10,000 words? Of course not! And the reason a two-year-old child should not have the objective imposed on him of achieving a 10,000-word vocabulary before his third birthday is that our knowledge of implicit distributional data (implicit *norms*) tells us that a vocabulary of that size would be preposterously large for a two-year-old.

HOW TO DEVELOP NORMS FOR CRITERION-REFERENCED TESTS

There is really no great trick to developing norms for criterion-referenced tests. It is done in exactly the same way as for tests that are *not* criterion-referenced—even though norms for the two categories of tests are not *used* in precisely the same way. As for the question of what *kind* of norms should be obtained, our preference is generally for some type of within-group referencing, such as that provided by *percentile norms,* rather than the type of between-groups referencing provided by norms of the grade-equivalent type. There are so many disadvantages to the use of grade equivalents and they result in so much misinterpretation, misunderstanding, and misuse that complete abandonment of the concept could result in a net gain. Although this book is perhaps not the proper forum for a disquisition on the hazards of grade equivalents, it may be a convenience to some readers, who may be unaware of the problems inherent in use of this type of normative data, to point out a few of these problems.

1. In almost any test of aptitude or achievement or developed abilities in school-related subjects the variability within grade is far greater than the difference between means of adjacent grades. It is often greater, as a matter of fact, than the difference between means of grades two or three years apart. Thus what appears in terms of grade equivalents to be a very superior (or inferior) performance may in actuality be quite unexceptional.

Comparison with percentile norms makes this quite apparent. Consider, for instance the Project TALENT Arithmetic Reasoning Test. Suppose this test were given to tenth-graders towards the beginning of April (in other words about seven-tenths of the way through the school year). Now let us consider two hypothetical students, both quite unexceptional. Student A gets a raw score of 7, which corresponds to a percentile of 45; student B gets a raw score of 8, which puts him at the 55th percentile. Both these percentiles are sufficiently close to 50 that it is clear that they represent quite average performance. In Project TALENT grade equivalents were never used, since their deficiencies were fully realized. But if they *had* been used a raw score of 7 would have been reported as a grade equivalent of 9.6, which makes it appear that student A is more than a full year behind where he should be in April of his tenth grade (grade 10.7). Student B, on the other hand, would appear to have achieved enough to be in the eleventh grade; his grade equivalent would be 11.1. The percentile values, 45 and 55, clearly give a much better idea of where students A and B stand in their arithmetic reasoning ability than would grade equivalents that would suggest that one student is fully a year and a half ahead of the other in his skills in this area.

2. Grade-equivalent norms are often based on data obtained at only one point in the school year; for instance end-of-year testing. Thus while the grade equivalents 4.9, 5.9, 6.9, etc. may be based on firm empirical data, all the in-between values (5.3, 6.1, etc.) will be based on interpolation, often using the highly questionable assumption that growth is linear throughout the year. In school subjects growth is quite likely to slow up during the summer months, and for some students an actual loss is likely during that period. (Some forgetting occurs.) What, then, would be the proper grade equivalent to assign to a score that represents the typical performance of students at the grade 7.8 level (end of April) and also represents the typical performance of students at the grade 8.0 level (the following September) but is lower than the typical level at grade 7.9 (end of May)? There is no sensible answer to this question.

3. Empirical data for normative purposes are seldom obtained outside the range of grades in which the test is intended for use, but the scores will almost certainly cover a considerably wider range of "grade equivalents." This means that extrapolation of the empirical data is necessary—and extrapolation is even more likely to be misleading than interpolation is. As a matter of fact, in the case of a test on a school subject, extrapolated grade equivalents that go beyond the range in which the subject is taught are essentially meaningless. But they *look* as if they mean something—and that is their real danger!

4. In using grade-equivalent norms there is usually a tacit understanding—or to be somewhat more precise, a tacit *mis*understanding— that growth either is or should be at the same uniform rate for all children.

5. Somewhat related to this, though not quite the same, is the tacit assumption that a year of growth at one grade level is equal to a year of growth at any other—for instance that the difference between grade equivalents 10.8 and 11.8 in reading represents the same amount of improvement, or growth, or learning, as the difference between grade equivalents 1.1 and 2.1. This assumption is quite unjustified. It is not even possible to get agreement as to what is *meant* by the statement that two amounts of change are the same— much less to *demonstrate* equality in a specific situation.

For further discussion of what is wrong with grade equivalents see Horst, Tallmadge, and Wood (1974, pp. 9–10), or Tallmadge and Horst (1974, pp. 79–92).

HOW TO USE NORMS FOR CRITERION-REFERENCED TESTS

Norms for criterion-referenced tests are used much as norms for norm-referenced tests are—to evaluate the performance of examinees with reference to the standard group on whom the norms are based. But they may also be used for another purpose for which norms on tests that lack the criterion-referencing feature cannot. This additional use is as a means of evaluating the norms group itself.

Consider, for instance, a 60-item vocabulary test that is not criterion-referenced. If the mean score for a norms group consisting of a representative sample of all high-school seniors in the United States is 39.0, that tells nothing whatever about the size of vocabulary typical of seniors. One has to know something about the test content to be able to draw inferences of that sort. And if one *does* know something about the test content, one's knowledge about it may range anywhere from the least precise sort of information—a vague impression, possibly derived from a casual look at the test— to the most precise sort of information, namely domain-referenced information. Suppose, for instance, that the 60-item vocabulary test consists of multiple-choice items testing knowledge of a representative sample of all the adjectives in a specified edition of a specified abridged dictionary; and suppose further that the test has been carefully developed in accordance with a carefully developed rationale including detailed specifications, and that the scores are properly corrected for chance, so that insofar as possible they provide a measure of mastery largely uncontaminated by the effects of guessing. If all those suppositions hold, the mean score of 39.0 stands by itself as a meaningful piece of information. It tells us that the average high-school senior understands about 65% of the adjectives in the specified standard reference work (i.e. the specified dictionary); in other words, the 39.0 mean indicates 65% mastery of the domain.

It should be recognized that for the purpose of evaluating *individuals* (as opposed to *groups*) norms are probably considerably more useful for domain-referenced tests than for objective-referenced tests. For objective-referenced tests, the norms provide group information, and groups that have been tested can be compared with the norms groups. However, as far as individuals are concerned, one is primarily interested in defining them as "pass" or "fail" (or whatever other dichotomy is being used to designate those certifiable as meeting the objective and those not certifiable)—rather than in attaching to each individual a number that identifies his percentile.

5
Using criterion-referenced tests

In this chapter we are concerned primarily, but not exclusively, with criterion-referenced tests of the objective-referenced type—in other words with tests on which some standard of performance has been set, which the examinees either meet or fail to meet.

CATEGORIES OF USES OF CRITERION-REFERENCED TESTS

Uses of criterion-referenced tests in schools fall in two main categories: (1) to evaluate individuals or groups (i.e. to determine where they stand at any particular time), and (2) to evaluate curricula or programs of instruction (i.e. to determine what sorts of growth or learning or other changes they produce). These two categories may be further subdivided according to whether the evaluation is summative or formative in character. Thus a somewhat more complete categorization of the uses of criterion-referenced tests in schools would be as follows:

I. *Evaluation of status* (with respect to mastery of the domain, or achievement of the objectives with which the test is concerned).
   A. Evaluation of the achievement of individuals or groups for diagnostic purposes (formative evaluation).
      1. Identifying the strengths, weaknesses, and specific needs of the group (e.g. the class).
      2. Identifying the strengths, weaknesses, and needs of the individual student (e.g. for individualized instruction).
   B. Overall evaluation of the achievement of individuals or groups (summative evaluation).
      1. Evaluating the group to determine their level of mastery.
      2. Evaluating the achievement of the individual student (for instance for use in placement or to prescribe next steps).

Table 5-1. Some Uses of Criterion-referenced Tests.

Purpose	Situation	What or Who Is Being Evaluated	Kind of C.R. Test	Reason for Test	Variable of Primary Interest
1. Evaluation of students	1. Individualized instruction or some form of self-pacing is used; or else, in the case of a conventional (nonindividualized) program, a criterion-referenced standard may have been set for passing the course.	1. The student	1. Objective-referenced or domain-referenced	1a. To determine whether the individual has achieved mastery of the unit or module and is ready to proceed to the next one *or* consider this particular phase of his education completed.	1a. Score upon completion of a unit.
				1b. To find out what progress the student is making toward mastery, at various stages in his work on the unit.	1b. Score at various states in the student's work on the unit.

2. Placement of students	2. Multiple classes or grades or levels are available. The most appropriate placement is to be made.	2. The student	2. Objective-referenced or or domain-referenced	2. To find the class or level most appropriate for the student.	2. Score before the unit has started.
3. Evaluation of instructional approach	3. The effectiveness of a particular educational program or teaching methodology is being evaluated.	3. The educational program	3. Objective-referenced or domain-referenced	3a. To determine whether the students are achieving mastery.	3a. Score before the unit has started and score upon completion.
				3b. To demonstrate that the students have achieved mastery.	3b. Score upon completion of unit.

(continued)

Table 5-1 (continued)

Purpose	Situation	What or Who Is Being Evaluated	Kind of C.R. Test	Reason for Test	Variable of Primary Interest
4. Comparative evaluation of different instructional approaches	4. Two different instructional methods are being compared to see which one produces mastery more quickly.	4. Instructional programs	4. Objective-referenced or domain-referenced	4. To obtain distributional data on time to mastery.	4. Mean time for the members of the group to achieve mastery under a particular instructional method.
5. Evaluation of individuals with respect to a particular domain	5. [Not necessarily related to school]	5. The individual	5. Domain-referenced	5. To determine the individual's level of mastery of the domain.	5. Absolute score (domain-referenced score) at time of test.

Using criterion-referenced tests

II. *Evaluation of change.*
  A. Determination of the effectiveness of a particular curriculum, procedure, program, teaching method, etc., for a group or individual.
  B. Determination of the relative effectiveness of various procedures, programs, curricula, etc.

Table 5-1 shows some of the uses of criterion-referenced tests (in a slightly different organization from that shown above, to provide a different perspective), along with characteristic features of each such use.

It should be noted that category I above (evaluation of status) may require only a single administration of the test, if one is interested in status at just one particular time, whereas category II (evaluation of change) necessarily requires administration of the test at least twice (although presumably, as we shall see, a different form is administered on each occasion).

SETTING THE STANDARD OF COMPETENCE

The concept of "standard of competence"

For each examinee on a criterion-referenced test there is a competence level (percentage of all possible items in the domain to which he knows the answer) and a score (percentage of test items he answers correctly, in a random sample of all possible items). Corresponding to these, if the criterion-referenced test is of the type sometimes called objective-referenced, a standard of competence that examinees are to meet and a cutting score on the test are set.

Table 5-2 shows the relation of these four numbers—competence level, test score, standard of competence, and cutting score—to one another.

The standard of competence is an arbitrary standard of achievement or accomplishment that has been set for some "domain" of knowledge. For instance, suppose the standard is set at 80%. That means that if there is good reason to believe a person has mastered 80% of the *entire* domain (not just 80% of that sample of the domain that was included in the criterion-referenced test), he will be certified to have achieved the established standard of mastery, or

Table 5-2. Relation of Mastery of Item Sample Constituting the Test to Mastery of Population of Items Constituting the Domain.

		ENTIRE DOMAIN	TEST (Sample of domain)
No. of items ⟶		Probably either infinite or a large finite number. However, it may occasionally be a rather small number.	Usually a moderate or small number
Percentages of items mastered	Examinee	*Examinee's competence level* (= percentage of items the examinee would be capable of answering correctly)	*Examinee's test score* (= percentage of items answered correctly)
	Cutting point defining the lowest satisfactory score	*Standard of competence* (usually set quite arbitrarily)	*Cutting score* (= "passing mark")

to have passed the examination; and that therefore, in view of this accomplishment, he will be entitled to all the perquisites pertaining thereunto. What those perquisites are will depend on the nature of the domain, the kind of person to whom the examination applies, and other characteristics of the situation. For instance, for an elementary-school student in some kind of individualized instruction program, the test may be designed to determine whether he has mastered a particular module or unit of instruction, and may therefore proceed to the next one. Or a set of examinations may be used for course placement of a student—for instance to determine whether a student who has studied analytic geometry by himself and has had no formal instruction in it has mastered the concepts he will need in calculus well enough to be permitted to skip the analytic geometry course and go directly into a calculus course.

A person's competence level does not necessarily coincide with his score on the criterion-referenced test since the test does not consist of all possible items in the domain, but merely of a presumably random sample of them.

The cutting score, which is discussed later in this chapter, is used operationally. The standard of competence, however, is considered conceptually, but can never be used operationally—for exactly the same reason that the examinee's test score can be determined operationally while his competence level can only be estimated.

Nevertheless it is important to decide what the standard of competence should be—and not just because this standard of competence is relevant in setting the cutting score (as discussed in the next section). Explicitly setting a standard of competence also helps insure that the authorities administering the test and using the results operationally have thought through the question of *why* they are using the test and what they are trying to do with it. The standard of competence to be set is not a function of the test itself but of the nature of the subject-matter area covered (the domain) and the purpose for which the test is being used.

How the standard of competence is set: the role of norms

The decision as to what an appropriate standard of competence is may be based on formal research (although this is seldom done) or on impressions derived from relevant experience (experience in teaching, for instance). The standard of competence is the level required in order to be able to do or understand or cope with whatever it is that the materials on which achievement is being assessed are intended to prepare one to do or understand or cope with. It should be noted in this connection that the experience of a knowledgeable and expert teacher is by no means an inadequate substitute for formal research. Value judgments are an important component of any decision of this sort—and value judgments are necessarily based in large part on considerations other than research results.

But regardless of whether formal research is undertaken prior to establishing the standard or, on the other hand, it is set on the basis of vague impressions as to what is reasonable, norms, in one way or another, enter the picture. Even if precise and explicit normative data are not consulted, and if, instead, the standard of competence is established on the basis of other knowledge, that other knowledge will inevitably, consciously or unconsciously, take into account some sort of normative data, perhaps fairly accurate, perhaps badly inaccurate—but in one way or another the concept of norms will have an effect.

For instance, why should instruction in reading be started at about age 6 (or age 5, or age 7, depending on what expert one happens to be getting advice from)? The answer is that age 6 (or 5, or 7) is the age at which the *typical child* is believed to be ready to learn to read—in other words capable of this type of learning. The concept of "typical child" implies the concept of norms.

Or consider the problem of licensing physicians. What the candidate is expected to know is clearly based on normative data. Physicians are certainly expected to know how to diagnose acute appendicitis, and to know the proper way of handling it. But they are not expected to know how to treat a color-blind person to give him normal color vision, or how to cure any disease for which at present there is no known cure. Not requiring candidates for licensure as physicians to know how to achieve these cures does not mean it would not be desirable for them to have these abilities; it merely means that they do not, and that this fact is recognized. "Normative data" indicate that zero percent of physicians can cure what is currently incurable.

The "mastery level" concept

Some writers on criterion-referenced tests use the term "mastery level" for what we are calling "standard of competence." However, we agree with Davis and Diamond (1974) that the term "mastery" should be reserved for 100% mastery.

A child has not "mastered" the elements of multiplication (of single-digit numbers) if he continues to think that $9 \times 3 = 26$; the fact that he knows the other 54 of the 55[1] pairs of one-digit numbers (all digits from 0 through 9) does not mean that "mastery" has been achieved. With this level of accomplishment complete mastery is probably just around the corner but it has not quite been reached. And surely nobody would want to claim that a child has "mastered" the alphabet because he could recognize 24 out of the 26 letters (in other words over 90% of the letters). This is clearly an instance where a 90% level is not good enough.

Thus there are some skills and sets of information for which the standard should be set at 100%, with perhaps some very small allowance for clerical error—error of the type that might occur, for instance, in a four-choice multiple-choice item, through marking B on the answer sheet, when one knows very well that the answer is D. This kind of clerical inaccuracy does occur occasionally. And if clerical accuracy does not happen to be the function the test is designed to measure, some appropriate allowance might be made for it—perhaps a 2% or 3% error rate but certainly not much more.

Thus in the situation of the multiplication test cited above, if the examinee gave 26 as the answer to the 9×3 problem but would state the answer to be 27 when asked, or would answer correctly on retest, it would be reasonable to assume that his initial wrong answer was due to a "slip of the pencil," or something very much like that, and mastery could then be assumed.

But not every objective for which a criterion-referenced test is developed demands 100% mastery. For some, a considerably lower rate may be quite acceptable for some purposes. Consider, for example, reading comprehension. It is the rare reader indeed who habitually extracts 100% of the meaning from everything he reads. He may extract quite enough of the meaning to serve his immediate purposes, but, particularly if he is employing a skimming mode of reading, *complete* extraction of all the information, implications, subtle hints, broad generalizations, and moods that the passage is intended to convey, as well as the critical evaluation processes that would permit the reader to make an appropriate decision as to the value of what he is reading—its probable accuracy and soundness, and its general merit—is unlikely. Some standard substantially below 100% would almost certainly be reasonable. Perhaps 80% or 75% or even considerably less would be deemed reasonable for certain purposes and for certain types of test items, based on certain types of reading materials.

SETTING THE CUTTING SCORE

As has already been indicated, the appropriate cutting score expressed in terms of percentage of correct answers is not necessarily the same as the standard of competence that has been set (which of course is also expressed in terms of percentage of the domain that must be mastered). For instance, if it has been decided that mastery of 80% of the *domain* is needed, the passing mark on the criterion-referenced test should not necessarily be set at 80% correct.

If we accept this assertion that the optimum cutting point on the test does not necessarily correspond to the standard of competence set for the entire domain, this leaves us with two auxiliary questions:

1. Should the cutting point be set at the same level for everybody? More specifically, should it be the same for the student who has not taken the course (or studied the module) and wishes to be exempted from it as for the student who has completed the course?

2. If the cutting point is not to be set to correspond exactly to the established standard of mastery, where should it be set, and why?

This entire matter, including the mathematics of the solution, is discussed fully in Appendix A. Therefore we shall just summarize the findings here.

The findings are a little bit surprising. It turns out that the more competent the group as a whole, the *lower* the cutting score may be set. Thus if a pretest is being given to determine which examinees have achieved a sufficiently high level of competence to be exempted from a particular course, the cutting score should be set higher than it is for the posttest administered upon completion of the course. This is the finding when the aim is to find the cutting score that will minimize misclassifications (false passes and false failures).

Thus while a cutting score of 80% may work quite well for a group consisting of individuals who have had a full quota of instruction, perhaps it should be 100% for individuals lacking the formal instruction and seeking an exemption of some sort.

It should be noted that these somewhat paradoxical results apply to an even greater extent when the test is of the constructed-answer type (open-end or completion questions) than when it is multiple choice; thus chance success is not an important factor in accounting for the paradox.

The chief source of the paradoxical findings is the fact that as a result of "sampling errors," the small sample of items that constitute the test may not be a truly representative sample of the infinite or large finite number of potential items constituting the domain. The magnitude of the phenomenon depends jointly on a number of considerations:

1. The number of items in the test.

2. Whether the items are of the constructed-answer type or the multiple-choice type; and if the latter, how many options per item there are.

3. The nature of the distribution of competence levels in the group to be tested.

4. How high the standard of competence has been set.

5. The relative seriousness of the two kinds of misclassifications: false passes and false failures. This is almost always a value judgment, rather than a question that can be decided on the basis of objective evidence.

The finding that to minimize misclassification the cutting score should be set higher when the test is administered *before* instruction than when it is administered after instruction may have considerable practical significance in the application of criterion-referenced tests. Readers who wish to apply this finding in setting cutting scores on tests for use for specific purposes with specific groups are advised to study carefully Tables A-5 and A-6 in Appendix A. These tables should provide guidance as to where to set the cutting scores.

SITUATIONS WHERE REPEATED TESTINGS ARE REQUIRED

Evaluation of an educational program, method, or curriculum

As is indicated in Table 5-1 (last column, row 3a) when a criterion-referenced test is used to evaluate the effectiveness of an educational program of some sort, both a pretest and a posttest are needed. It is not enough to know that the students are performing well at the end of the course; perhaps they would have scored well at the beginning. It is necessary, therefore, to be able to demonstrate that some improvement has occurred.

Other situations requiring repeated testing

Requiring more than one administration of a test may be the norm (the word ''norm'' is used here in its nontechnical sense) rather than the exception, when criterion-referenced tests are used in a school situation. For instance when a predetermined standard of competence has been established corresponding to a particular behavioral objective, the student may be tested repeatedly until his score is such that he can be certified to have met the standard.

Handling repeated testing

In some situations where repeated testings are required—either in a pretest-posttest situation or because students have to be retested until they are able to pass (i.e. to meet the standard of competence)—the same form of the same test is administered repeatedly. This can completely defeat the purpose of the testing. The items no longer represent the entire domain of which they are supposed to be a sample; instead they *become* a complete domain themselves—a very limited one, but nevertheless the one that students may concentrate on mastering. In other words if a student who is having difficulty learning a particular topic (or ''mastering a particular behavioral objective'') discovers that in order to be certified to have reached the specified standard of competence all he has to do is to memorize the answers to a small number of test items

Using criterion-referenced tests

that he has already seen—perhaps several times—he will concentrate on memorizing those answers, so that the test score becomes meaningless. And even if he conscientiously tries to learn and understand the material with which the test items deal, rather than depending on rote memory, passing the test will merely signify that he has mastered the subject matter covered by the test and will indicate absolutely nothing about the domain as a whole that it is supposed to represent.

Therefore multiple forms of the test are *absolutely essential* in most situations where retesting may be required. There are only two exceptions:

> 1. When the test is a noncognitive one, for which memorization could not be a factor, and for which practice effect is either nonexistent or negligible.
> 2. When the test is identical with the domain—in other words when the test items are not merely a small sample of the items that constitute the domain, but instead are a 100% sample. (One example might be a test to measure recognition of the capital and small letters of the alphabet. This domain consists of 52 potential items. If all 52 are included it is obviously not only unnecessary but impossible to construct a separate parallel form)

As might be inferred from paragraph 2 above, when the domain (the universe of potential items) is finite in magnitude, the larger the proportion of items sampled the less the need for parallel forms.

But when parallel forms of a test *are* to be constructed, it is of course essential, as indicated in Chapter 3, that they be genuine, independently constructed parallel forms, rather than trivial variants of the original form. In other words the parallel form should not be constructed to be parallel item by item, because this would make it and the initial form spuriously alike. Instead each new form must be based on a brand-new sampling of content from the curriculum (or from whatever else defines the domain). The only exception—in other words the only circumstances under which different forms should be parallel item by item—is when the test specifications define the test content item by item. This is tantamount to stratified sampling from the domain, with the strata being defined so narrowly that the items in a stratum differ only trivially.

Effect on teaching: the teaching-to-the-test problem

The undesirability of teaching to the test and the necessity of avoiding it were discussed in Chapter 3. However, it seems desirable to resume the discussion at this point since teaching to the test is most likely to occur when the same form of the same test is administered and readministered repeatedly to the same student until the preestablished cutting score is reached or exceeded. Teaching to the test is still a danger even when legitimate parallel forms of the test are available and used, but it is to some extent a lesser danger, since the teacher would have to teach to *all* forms of the test thereby getting at least a little closer to teaching to the universe, in other words teaching the entire domain. But just as there is one circumstance in which parallel forms of the test are neither needed nor possible (i.e. when the test coincides with the domain), it should be noted that the same circumstance justifies (indeed, it demands) ''teaching to the test.'' In other words there is nothing wrong with ''teaching to the test''—in fact that is exactly what should be done—*if* the test happens to coincide with the universe of items rather than merely sampling from it. For instance let us again consider the objective of being able to recognize all the letters of the alphabet. If the test has 52 items, one for each capital and lower-case letter, *of course* the teacher should teach all 52 items even though that could be regarded by some as ''teaching to the test.'' But suppose one is foolish enough to use a six-item test, testing for recognition of the letters B, F, H, M, U, and Y, and that one is also foolish enough to teach to *this* test. The result, children who could recognize the six selected capital letters perfectly but who might have considerable trouble with some of the other 20, and with all 26 lower-case letters, is certainly not what is sought.

USING CRITERION-REFERENCED TESTS FOR FORMATIVE AND SUMMATIVE EVALUATIONS (OF INDIVIDUALS, GROUPS, AND PROGRAMS)

Formative evaluations

Criterion-referenced tests may be used for diagnostic purposes; in other words to identify the strengths, weaknesses, and specific needs both of the individual students and the group as a whole (e.g. the class). When used in this manner, the test results can provide a basis for helping decide what direction subsequent instruction shall take—what modifications in emphasis or methods may be desirable.

Summative evaluations
Summative evaluations of individuals and groups

Criterion-referenced tests may be used for overall evaluation, with respect both to individual students and to the group as a whole. When used for individuals they operate in the pass-fail context, to determine whether the standard has been met and whether the student may therefore proceed to the next stage. When used for groups (classes, schools, cities, states, etc.) there is generally some normative connotation.

Evaluation of an innovative program or curriculum

As was indicated at the beginning of this chapter, criterion-referenced tests may be used to evaluate group (or individual) performance in the context of program evaluation. It is worth pointing out, in this connection, that when evaluating an innovative program it is not enough just to demonstrate that learning or growth occurs in some significant amount—in other words that the posttest scores are significantly better than the pretest scores; it is also necessary to demonstrate cost-effectiveness. Thus if the costs (including both monetary and other costs) are equal for the innovative program and whatever it is supposed to replace, it is necessary to show that the learning or other benefits to be derived from the innovative program are at least as great as those from the status quo. And if the costs (monetary and other) of the innovative program are greater than the status quo costs, it is necessary to show that the benefits are at least correspondingly greater.

Furthermore some instructional programs are in fields in which maturation can be expected to occur in the normal course of events; in other words some learning or growth will take place even without formal instruction. In evaluating an instructional program in such a field, some provision has to be made for this possibility, so that gains due to maturation will not be confused with gains attributable to the educational program. A person's vocabulary, for instance, is likely to grow throughout his lifetime, whether or not he is in an educational program in which formal instruction aimed at vocabulary enlargement is provided.

SCORING MULTIPLE-CHOICE TESTS

The score on a criterion-referenced test can be expressed either in raw-score terms (number of items) or, preferably, in whatever metric corresponds to the absolute meaning of the score. The absolute-meaning metric, for many criterion-referenced tests, is a percentage score (percentage of items to which the answer is known) from which percentage of the domain mastered is inferred. But on many tests score is reported as percentage (or number) of items answered correctly. This practice is very misleading and generally undesirable when the test is of the multiple-choice type[2] rather than the constructed-answer type. With multiple-choice tests, unless the test administration or processing procedure absolutely guarantees that, one way or another, every examinee will provide an answer to every item, it is extremely important that scores, whether in terms of number of items or percentage of items, be corrected for chance success in the conventional way. Even for tests that are not criterion-referenced, correcting multiple-choice scores for chance is highly desirable whenever the procedure is such that not everyone answers every item, because the correction procedure improves the validity of the scores. But it is *especially* important for criterion-referenced tests, because only if the correction is made is there any basis for assuming that the percentage score is a reasonable estimate of percentage of the domain mastered (i.e. percentage of the domain of items *to which the answer is known,* as opposed to the somewhat larger percentage answered correctly). If scores are not corrected for chance there is no sensible way of generalizing from score to domain, and if this cannot be done there is no point in calling the test "criterion-referenced."

As was pointed out in Chapter 3, even tests of the constructed-answer type are not necessarily guess-free. However, scores on

Using criterion-referenced tests

them are not nearly as subject to distortion resulting from the failure to apply a correction for guessing as scores on multiple-choice tests are; and besides, there is no correction formula applicable to constructed-answer tests.

The conventional correction-for-chance formula for multiple-choice scores expressed in terms of number of items is:

$$K = R - \frac{W}{n-1} \quad (1)$$

where K = corrected score
      = estimated number of answers known
   R = number of items answered correctly
   W = number of items answered incorrectly (this does not include omitted items)
   n = number of options per item

The corresponding formula for scores expressed in terms of percentage of items is:

$$K_p = 100 \frac{K}{N} \quad (2)$$

where K_p = corrected score expressed as a percentage of items
   N = number of items in test
   K has the same definition as for formula 1 above

Both of these correction formulas assume that wrong answers are due to guessing. In recommending use of these formulas we are of course under no illusion that the assumption is uniformly true. Partial information is a factor, and so is *misinformation*. In the latter category, consider the following spelling item, in which the task is to decide which of the options if any is the correct spelling:

   A. seeze.
   B. sieze.
   C. seze.
   *D. seize.
   E. none of the above.

Examinees who trust the widely believed but very undependable spelling rule "*i* before *e* except after *c*" are very likely to pick option B. They will not be guessing; their error will be due to misinformation.

The widely held belief that correction for guessing is of no importance at all except for speeded tests is totally without foundation. As long as some examinees fail to answer some items the correction formula helps cancel out the resulting inequity. It does not matter at all what the examinee's reasons for not answering every item are; he may omit some items because he does not have time to reach them, or because he lacks confidence in himself, or because he has been indoctrinated against guessing and somewhere along the line has been led to believe that it is immoral to answer a test item when one is not absolutely certain of the answer. Whatever the explanation of the omitted items, the examinee who does the omitting is at a disadvantage if no adjustment is made in the scores of those who tend to answer every item regardless of whether they know the correct answer or just guess. Instructing examinees to answer every item, as a means of making the correction for guessing unnecessary, does not work very satisfactorily. In the first place, to the extent that this instruction is followed the reliability of the scores is impaired. And in the second place, no matter how emphatically the instruction not to omit any items is presented, some examinees will fail to follow it—either because they do not finish or because they have been so effectively indoctrinated in the past to "avoid wild guessing."

Many test developers and test users are of the opinion that correcting scores for chance is too complicated and too difficult to use as a standard procedure. The author of this book disagrees. In the first place even with hand-scoring, the correction computation, when executed with an efficient procedure, takes hardly any longer than using the uncorrected score. (When a computerized procedure is used, correcting for chance requires no more effort than not correcting; but probably the vast majority of criterion-referenced tests used in the classroom are hand-scored.) Moreover, a very slight increase in time required for scoring is an infinitesimal price to pay for substantially increased validity of the scores, supplemented, in the case of criterion-referenced tests, by substantially more accurate criterion-referencing (i.e. substantially more meaningful scores in absolute terms).

More sophisticated and very slightly more precise scoring formulas, involving "choice-weighted scoring" (Davis, 1967), are feasible when the scoring is to be done by computer, but the improvement they provide is too slight to warrant the added complications and added cost when hand-scoring is necessary. In the latter situation, as Davis (1967) points out, the conventional correction formula provides the best compromise between convenience and precision, sacrificing hardly any of either.

NOTES

[1] The count 55 is based on the assumption that the commutative principle has been mastered—in other words, that it is known that $7 \times 2 = 2 \times 7$. If this assumption is not made the count would be 100, not 55.

[2] The term "multiple-choice" is used in this context to apply not only to tests composed of items in the traditional multiple-choice format, but also to true-false tests, matching-items tests, and other objective-item formats in which the examinee chooses from two or more options.

6
Evaluating criterion-referenced tests

This book began with the statement that there is an enormous amount of confusion about criterion-referenced measurement. We have now reached the part where it should be pointed out that a very large proportion of the confusion that has been generated and the misconceptions that have gotten into print as a consequence have to do with the *evaluation* of criterion-referenced tests. It is commonly but erroneously thought, for instance, that standard test theory (including concepts of validity coefficients, reliability coefficients, etc.) is largely inapplicable to criterion-referenced tests. A fairly typical exposition of this belief, by Popham and Husek (1969), follows:

> The issue of variability is at the core of the difference between norm-referenced and criterion-referenced tests. Since the meaningfulness of a norm-referenced score is basically dependent on the relative position of the score in comparison with other scores, the more variability in the scores the better. With a norm-referenced test, we want to be able to tell Jamie from Joey from Frank, and we feel more secure about telling them apart if their scores are very different.
>
> With criterion-referenced tests, variability is irrelevant. The meaning of the score is not dependent on comparison with other scores; it flows directly from the connection between the items and the criterion. It is, of course, true that one almost always gets variant scores on any psychological test; but that variability is not a necessary condition for a good criterion-referenced test.
>
> The subtle and not-so-subtle implications of this central difference in the relevance of variability must permeate any discussion of the two approaches to testing. For example, we all have been told that a

Evaluating criterion-referenced tests

> test should be reliable and valid. We have all read about test construction and item analysis. The procedures may not always be simple, the formulas may not be trivial; but there are hundreds of books and thousands of articles to guide us. Unfortunately, most of what these "helpmates" outline as "good" things to do are not only irrelevant to criterion-referenced tests, but are actually injurious to their proper development and use. This is true because the treatments of validity, the suggestions about reliability, and the formulas for item analysis are all based on the desirability of variability among scores. The connection may not be obvious but it is always there.

This is quoted not through any desire to imply that its authors are the sole proponents of the viewpoint expressed in the quotation, but because it so beautifully encapsulates the elements of what seems currently to be the most widely prevalent view.

The passage quoted may sound quite reasonable when one first encounters it. Actually, though, it sets up a straw man, by imputing a very narrow meaning to some of the major concepts of standard test theory and then asserting, quite correctly, that these *narrow* meanings are not applicable to criterion-referenced tests. But if one interprets standard test theory in its most general context, it is just as applicable to criterion-referenced tests as to norm-referenced tests. In the sections that follow we shall see how this works.

First of all, though, let us consider why we use achievement tests at all—in other words why we use measurement instruments. We do it because we have reason to believe that the instruments will show up differences—in other words that not everybody in the group for which the test is appropriate will always get the same score. We do not have special clocks that tell us which hours contain 73 minutes and which hours contain 44 minutes; we have no need for such clocks because all hours every day have exactly 60 minutes. By the same token it would not be necessary to administer achievement tests if we knew without the use of such tests that all the students were learning at the same rate and that by the time a specified period had elapsed all of them would have mastered the material of the course (or unit, or module) perfectly. But of course we have no such assurance. Therefore, our first action should be to stop and think. *What is the group of scores we are interested in? Among whom (or what) are we interested in differentiating? What is the reason for the test?* Depending on the situation, the answer might be found in one of the rows of Table 6-1.

The observant reader will note that Table 6-1 bears a striking resemblance to Table 5-1. In fact the first six columns of Table 6-1, which relate to operational use of the criterion-referenced test in various contexts, recapitulate Table 5-1. The remaining columns show the kind of data needed to evaluate the test's effectiveness. As in Table 5-1, the first four rows of Table 6-1 refer to school-related applications or to applications to some form of formal educational program. The fifth row is not thus limited. It will be observed that in the case of the school-related applications (i.e. rows 1–4 of the table) scores for use in evaluating the test's reliability, validity, and accuracy[1] must be obtained more than once. This is true even, for instance, where the *operational* use of the test calls for obtaining criterion-referenced scores just once.

In situation 1 we are not interested in finding a spread in scores among students who have completed the unit and have therefore achieved mastery. (We know that those who have completed the unit have achieved mastery because that is the definition of ''completing the unit.'') We do want to know, however, how well the test differentiates between those who have studied the unit and those who have not yet had that experience. In row 1a we present a situation where only posttest scores are available. Row 1b covers the somewhat more desirable situation where scores are available at numerous stages throughout the unit. Regardless of whether the 1a or 1b version of the situation is applicable, students who already have achieved mastery of the unit at pretest time presumably should not be subjected to the unit (assuming, of course, that the content of the criterion-referenced test validly represents what is taught in it). In any event if the test does not differentiate between those who have completed the unit and those who have not yet begun it, what is the reason for the test? And even more importantly, under those circumstances *what would be the reason for the instructional units?*

This brings us to situation 2, placement of students. If a test is intended for use in course placement, there clearly is an expectation that the students will differ in their pretest scores and that a student's pretest score indicates from what course he or she will profit most. It is for this reason that in evaluating the test we should know something about posttest as well as pretest.

Evaluating criterion-referenced tests 83

In situation 3 the criterion-referenced test is being used to evaluate an instructional program—to make certain it is working. Here, too, and for exactly the same reasons, it is important that the test differentiate between those who have had the instruction and those who have not—or, better yet, that it differentiate among those who have had varying amounts of instruction.

In situation 4 the criterion-referenced test is being used to *compare* different instructional programs, to determine which one is working better. The variable we are interested in, therefore, is the mean posttest score[2] for the program. This measure is needed for each program, for comparable groups.

We shall return to Table 6-1 later in this chapter, when we discuss how to determine the reliability of a criterion-referenced test and how to validate the test. One very important point that should be borne in mind throughout this discussion is that (contrary to what has been implied by many, and possibly most, writers on the evaluation of criterion-referenced tests[3]) there is nothing whatever in "classical" psychometric theory that limits its applicability to a single test administered at a single time to a lot of different people who have something in common—such as all the students in a particular grade. Classical psychometric theory (covering reliability, validity, item analysis, and other topics) is applicable to whatever sort of variable and whatever sort of group one wishes to apply it to. For instance it is applicable to sums of variables, difference scores, other linear composites, nonlinear functions of variables, time scores (amount of time to mastery), and just about whatever other sort of numerical scale one might wish to apply it to. It is applicable to dichotomous scales as well as continuous ones. And, as we shall see, *it is applicable to criterion-referenced scales as well as to norm-referenced ones.*

Ebel (1973) expresses a similar view. The final section of his article is headed "Statistics for Criterion-Referenced Tests," and it concludes with the following statement: "In view of these considerations we conclude that conventional test statistics are appropriate to criterion-referenced tests when they are based on appropriate test responses." (Ebel, 1973)

Carver (1974) makes an important distinction between two approaches, which he terms "psychometric procedures" and "edumetric procedures" respectively. The general principle he ad-

Table 6-1. Uses of Criterion-referenced Tests, for Which Test Evaluation May Be Needed.

		OPERATIONAL USE OF THE TEST		
Purpose	Situation	What or who is being evaluated	Kind of C.R. test	Reason for test
1. Evaluation of students	1. Individualized instruction or some form of self-pacing is used; or else, in the case of a conventional (nonindividualized) program, a criterion-referenced standard may have been set for passing the course.	1. The student	1. Objective-referenced or domain-referenced	1a. To determine whether the individual has achieved mastery of the unit or module and is ready to proceed to the next one or consider this particular phase of his education completed. 1b. To find out what progress the student is making toward mastery, at various stages in his work on the unit.
2. Placement of students	2. Multiple classes or grades or levels are available. The most appropriate placement is to be made.	2. The student	2. Objective-referenced or domain-referenced	2. To find the class or level most appropriate for the student.
3. Evaluation of instructional approach	3. The effectiveness of a particular educational program or teaching methodology is being evaluated.	3. The educational program	3. Objective-referenced or domain-referenced	3a. To determine whether the students are achieving mastery. 3b. To demonstrate that the students have achieved mastery.
4. Comparative evaluation of different instructional approaches	4. Two different instructional methods are being compared to see which one produces mastery more quickly.	4. Instructional programs	4. Objective-referenced or domain-referenced	4. To obtain distributional data on time to mastery.
5. Evaluation of individuals with respect to a particular domain	5. [Not necessarily related to school.]	5. The individual	5. Domain-referenced	5. To determine the individual's level of mastery of the domain.

[a] Separate forms of the test must be used each time unless the nature of the test is such that memory is not a factor and no differential practice effects can be expected.

	DATA NEEDED FOR EVALUATION OF TEST		
Variable of primary interest	Empirical validation[a]	Determine reliability[a]	Determining coefficient of accuracy[a]
1a. Score upon completion of a unit.	Initial score (pretest, before instruction) and final score (posttest).	Initial score, final score, and (optionally) scores at one or more intermediate points, on parallel forms of the test (two separate forms each time).	Same data as for coefficient or reliability, plus estimate of magnitude of absolute error.
1b. Score at various states in the student's work on the unit.	Initial score, final score, and (optionally) score at one or more intermediate points.		
2. Score before the unit has started.	Initial score (pretest) and final score (posttest).		
3a. Score before the unit has started and score upon completion.	Initial score (pretest), final score (posttest), and (optionally) score at one or more intermediate points.		
3b. Score upon completion of unit.	Initial score (pretest) and final score (posttest).		
4. Mean time for the members of the group to achieve mastery under a particular instructional method.	Initial score (pretest) and final score (posttest) for students in each of the programs being compared.		
5. Absolute score (domain-referenced score) at time of test.	[b]	Scores on parallel forms of test.	

[b] Empirical validation is seldom feasible in this situation. It becomes necessary to rely on content validity, which in turn requires knowledge of the method of test construction, population of items sampled, etc.

vocates is sound,[4] although the author of this book prefers to use the word "psychometric" in a broader and more inclusive sense than he does. In our usage the term "psychometric" includes any use of objective measurement or scaling, irrespective of whether the focus of interest is on status at a particular time or on amount and direction of change in a specified time period. This is the framework in which psychometric theory is set, or within which it is generally applicable. Thus the kinds of measures and procedures that Carver calls "edumetric" are subsumed, in our usage, under the more general heading "psychometric," obviating his neologism ("edumetric"). His conclusions, except for the matter of terminology, are essentially along the same lines as ours. It does seem to us, however, that there is a significant advantage in our broader and more inclusive definition of the term "psychometric"; the advantage lies in the unified framework it provides, with principles that apply to norm-referenced and criterion-referenced tests alike.

RELIABILITY

For tests to be used in a school-related context
(i.e. rows 1–4 of Table 6-1)
General considerations

It follows from the foregoing discussion and from an inspection of Table 6-1 that in one way or another most of the main uses of criterion-referenced tests, with the exception of row 5, which in general is not formally school-related, involve, either explicitly or (more likely) implicitly, a comparison between pretest and posttest scores, and an expectation that there will be a difference between them.

Recommended procedure

It follows from the discussion above that the set of scores with which we should be concerned in determining the reliability of a criterion-referenced test is the full range of scores extending from those who have no instruction in a unit or module corresponding to the objectives measured to those who have presumably completed the instructional program. This, of course, is somewhat different

Evaluating criterion-referenced tests

from the usual set of scores used in determining reliability of a norm-referenced test; what is usually used is scores for a large group of individuals in the same grade, all tested at the same time relative to the course of instruction (e.g. at the end of the course, the point for which the end-of-course test was designed). But nothing in classical psychometric theory says it is applicable only within a grade and for tests administered only at the end of the course.

If reliability is determined in the manner proposed above, covering the entire range, there are at least two ways it can be handled:

Procedure A. Using time elapsed as the dependent variable, and thus using as "scores" the time elapsed for specified percentages of mastery (e.g. 0%, 25%, 50%, 75%, and 100% mastery). (The percentage of mastery would thus be treated as the independent variable.)

Procedure B. Using raw score as the dependent variable, and using a few prespecified times of testing (not necessarily equally spaced) as the independent variable. For instance if 15 weeks were considered a reasonable period of instruction for most of the students the test might be administered six times—first as a pretest and then after the passage of 1, 3, 6, 10, and 15 weeks. Note that the successively longer periods between tests (or, to put it another way, the closer spacing of the earlier testings) would be advantageous in the not uncommon situation where the materials or skills being learned are such that a sharp drop-off in the rate of learning seems likely. If a somewhat steadier rate of learning until mastery is achieved seems likely, it might be preferable to space the six test administrations evenly—for instance a pretest followed by retesting after the passage of 3, 6, 9, 12, and 15 weeks.

Procedure B is probably preferable from a practical viewpoint (it is certainly simpler administratively) and it has no conspicuous theoretical disadvantages. If procedure B is used, the variance of the scores would have two independent components:

1. A component corresponding to intertime, intraindividual variance.

2. A component corresponding to interindividual, intratime variance.

The first of these components would probably be large in comparison with the second and thus would probably contribute substantially to the reliability of the instrument, while the second component might contribute only minimally.

In the quotation that appears at the beginning of this chapter, Popham and Husek suggest that because of lack of variability conventional concepts of test reliability are irrelevant. It should be noted that insofar as the argument about the possible absence of variability has any validity at all, it applies only to the second of the two components listed above; the first component *should* provide enough variability to produce a respectable reliability coefficient. If it does not, it is the fault of the test, or of the situation in which it is used; it is *not* the fault of the statistics. (We should not slay the messenger who brings bad news.)

In connection with the effect of absence of variability on a reliability coefficient or any other correlation coefficient, another prevalent misconception is worth mentioning at this point. It is widely, but erroneously, thought that if the standard deviation of either of the variables being correlated is exactly zero (in other words if everyone in the group is at the same point on that variable) the correlation is zero. That is not true. The reliability (or other correlation) under those circumstances is mathematically indeterminate (because it is equal to the indeterminate fraction 0/0). That just means that we do not know what the reliability is because we probably do not have an adequate or appropriate group on which to determine it—any more than we would be able to compute a correlation coefficient on just a single case. A genuine zero correlation occurs when the covariance between variables is zero but the standard deviations are nonzero. Thus if the standard deviations turn out to be zero it probably means a freakish or inappropriate situation of some kind. The point of all this disucssion is that the claim of some writers to the effect that scores on criterion-referenced tests have zero variability and that therefore normal concepts of reliability are inappropriate is completely invalid. It is quite true that for an extremely successful class or other group the end-of-course scores may all be 100%, and the reliability may therefore be indeterminate. But surely, as we have tried to make clear, the test must be intended for use with a wider group than that one highly and uniformly successful subgroup. If not, why test? Or why test with that particular test?

As for the actual details of computational procedure (assuming procedure B is used) let us define n and N as follows:

N = number of people on whom data are available
n = number of separate occasions on which person has been tested

For instance, if each person has been pretested and then retested after 1, 3, 6, 10, and 15 weeks, n equals 6. Likewise n would still equal 6 if retesting occurred after 3, 6, 9, 12, and 15 weeks—or after 5, 9, 12, 14, and 15 weeks; the spacing does not affect the procedure.

Let us further assume that two scores are obtained for each of the N persons on each of the n occasions. The two scores might be from parallel forms of the test or they might be split-half scores obtained from a single form.

The third possibility—the KR20 formula (Kuder and Richardson, 1937)—does not require a pair of scores on each occasion. But the conditions of item homogeneity and the other conditions it *does* require are much less likely to be met than the more modest requirements imposed by the parallel forms or split-half procedure. And the fourth possibility sometimes used for obtaining reliability coefficients, retest with the identical form, is almost *never* appropriate with paper-and-pencil tests of any kind—or, for that matter, with tests measuring any kinds of cognitive abilities or knowledge.[5]

In the unlikely event that the test is of such a nature that it is appropriate to use the same form of the test throughout, there will be n pairs of scores on the same form for each N persons (or nN pairs altogether). The simplest procedure is to treat each of the nN pairs as a separate "case" in computing the correlation coefficient.[6] Note that in this instance "case" is not synonymous with "person"; we have nN cases, but only N persons.

If a split-half reliability coefficient is being obtained it is suggested that instead of using the conventional Spearman-Brown formula to correct for test length, using Angoff formula 16 (Angoff, 1953) is preferable. This formula is:

$$r_{aa} = \frac{r_{12}\sigma_a^2}{(\sigma_1 + r_{12}\sigma_2)(\sigma_2 + r_{12}\sigma_1)}$$

where r_{aa} = "corrected" reliability coefficient for test A

r_{12} = raw correlation between "halves"

σ_1 and σ_2 = standard deviations for halves

σ_a = standard deviation for test A

For evaluation of individuals
(in or out of school) with respect to a particular domain
(i.e. row 5 of Table 6-1)

For a domain-referenced test to be used in this situation, direct computation of parallel-forms reliability is best. This, of course, requires the existence of parallel forms of the test.

An alternative procedure, split-half reliability, is available if the test is unspeeded and if it can be split into operationally independent halves each of which meets the test specifications separately.

Kuder-Richardson formula 20 (Kuder and Richardson, 1937), is a possibility if the assumptions underlying that formula happen to be met reasonably well by the test—but that is perhaps somewhat less likely for a domain-referenced test than for some norm-referenced tests.

A procedure that is *not* recommended
for reliability estimation

A method proposed by Livingston (1970, 1972) for determining a statistic to represent the "reliability" of criterion-referenced measures has gained considerable attention. Livingston proposes that for the purpose of working with data from criterion-referenced tests, variances (and covariances) be redefined to equal the mean of the squares (or cross-products) of deviations from the "*criterion score*" (i.e. from the cutting score) rather than of deviations from the mean. "Criterion-referenced correlations" are then defined in the same way as conventional product-moment correlations except that the *redefined* covariance is used in the numerator and the square root of the product of the *redefined* variances is used in the denominator. Then, just as the conventional reliability coefficient equals the square of the correlation between true score and obtained score, Livingston proposes to use as the reliability of a criterion-referenced test the square of the *criterion-referenced* correlation between true score and obtained score. Operationally he proposes computing parallel-forms reliability as the criterion-referenced correlation between parallel forms having the same criterion score.

Livingston's "CR reliability coefficient" may be a useful statistic for some kinds of applications, particularly with criterion-referenced tests of the objective-referenced type, scored dichotomously; but it probably should be given another name since it seems to be a measure of something other than "reliability."

As a measure of reliability the coefficient is flawed in several ways. In the first place the redefinition of the correlation coefficient and other statistics is purely arbitrary. Of course arbitrarily defined statistics are not necessarily *bad* statistics; after all, in a sense Karl Pearson arbitrarily defined the product-moment correlation coefficient, which has since then been shown to have many convenient mathematical properties, and consequently has proven both useful and durable. But in this case the results are not nearly so happy as they were with Pearson's invention. A major difficulty lies in the fact that the "criterion-referenced correlation coefficient" lacks essential properties of invariance. Although, like the Pearson r, it has $+1$ and -1 as its upper and lower bounds, unlike Pearson r it is not invariant under all linear transformations of the variables being correlated. A change in the cutting score (or a change in the location of the zero point *without* a corresponding change in the cutting score) can instantly change a "criterion-referenced reliability coefficient" from zero to as close to $+1$ as we wish to make it. As a matter of fact the more *inappropriately* the cutting score is set, the higher the "CR reliability coefficient" is likely to be.

VALIDITY

The ideal way of establishing the validity of *any* test is still to obtain its correlation with an appropriate external criterion. A criterion is fully "appropriate" if it meets the following three requirements:

    1. It must be relevant.

    2. Criterion measures must be uncontaminated by performance on the test being validated; and vice versa.

    3. The reliability of the criterion, though it need not be high, *should* be known (in order to permit correction of the validity coefficient for attenuation due to lack of perfect criterion reliability).

But for criterion-referenced achievement tests, as for norm-referenced achievement tests, and indeed for almost all other kinds of tests too, really good external criterion measures are not generally found lying around loose, waiting to be used; nor are they easy to develop. Fortunately in the case of achievement tests, whether norm-referenced or criterion-referenced, careful and skilled test construction, in conjunction with predetermined and very detailed test objectives, can usually establish the content validity of a test even though an adequate external criterion is not available.

Validation for evaluating the achievement of individuals or groups

As a matter of fact for most achievement tests, whether norm-referenced or criterion-referenced, content validity is the *only* kind of validation usually feasible. If a criterion-referenced test has been carefully and competently constructed in accordance with the principles discussed in Chapter 3, it will almost certainly have a high degree of content validity. Correlational validity (e.g. correlation with a concurrent criterion) is sometimes possible, and it will provide information as to the degree to which the test tends to rank people in the right order. But it will give no information whatever concerning the accuracy of the numbers that are supposed to indicate (in absolute terms) degree of mastery of the domain. Concern with the accuracy of scales in absolute rather than relative terms of course has no place in conventional test evaluation statistics—reliability, validity, etc.—since these statistics are normally expressed as a kind of correlation coefficient. It is well known that correlation coefficients are affected by relative placement of the cases but not by absolute placement of the scale. (The entire scale for a variable can be displaced by a constant amount throughout without having the slightest effect on correlation coefficients involving that variable.) This matter is discussed further in a later section of this chapter, "Accuracy."

Validation of a criterion-referenced test for use in evaluating the effectiveness of an educational program

One widely used definition of validity goes something like this:

> Validity is the degree to which an instrument measures that which it purports to measure (or predicts that which it purports to predict).

This definition implies the existence of a suitable criterion, either concurrent or predictive, with which test scores can be correlated. The prevalent misconception is to assume that in the case of a criterion-referenced test designed to find out whether the desired learning has taken place as a result of a course or an instructional program of some kind, the appropriate criterion is test score after the course has been completed. Usually it is not. What the appropriate criterion *is* depends to some extent on how the test is to be used—or in the terminology of the definition of validity presented above, what the test purports to measure. If the test is intended for evaluating the effectiveness of the course in producing the desired learning it should be administered to students who have not yet had the course and to students who have. The criterion against which score would be validated would be the dichotomy on whether the student had taken the course at the time he was tested. Or an alternative approach, replacing the dichotomous variable with a continuum, would be to administer the test at regular intervals throughout the course (using a different but parallel form each time). The criterion against which test score could be validated would then be time elapsed since the beginning of the course, or percentage of the course completed. (It should be recognized, of course, that the relationship might be nonlinear.)

Predictive validity

Much confusion has resulted from overlooking the distinction between "criterion-referenced tests," which generally provide *direct* measures of whether the criterion level of success has been achieved, and the entirely different sort of test represented by those whose function is to predict what will be achieved in the future, rather than to measure what has already been achieved. The importance of this distinction was suggested in Chapter 2. The point is brought up again in this chapter to emphasize that predictive validity is a meaningless concept when applied to criterion-referenced tests. Such tests have as their sole function *to describe the present situation* rather than to predict the future. Scores on the test may *happen* to be correlated with some future occurrence and thus may *happen* to predict it, but that was not the purpose of the test and that is not why it is being used. If it were, why would the criterion-referencing feature have been built into it? The "criterion" that is referred to in the term "criterion-referenced" is always a present condition; it is what the test *measures,* not what it predicts. In the case of predictive tests, where it is important to interpret results in terms of what they *predict,* rather than what they *directly measure,* the "criterion-referenced" approach (at least as the term is generally used) is usually inappropriate; as a matter of fact a good predictive test may be neither criterion-referenced nor norm-referenced. This point is not well understood.

ACCURACY

In the previous section the concept of "accuracy" in the sense of the precision with which the score represents *absolute* location (not merely location relative to other members of a group) on the scale corresponding to the objective or domain being measured was discussed.

It is here proposed that for criterion-referenced tests the concept of accuracy should be regarded as separate from and parallel to the twin concepts of reliability and validity. The author of this book has done some very preliminary work on this notion, and has derived some formulas relevant to it, which are presented in Appendix B. The reader should be forewarned, however, that the entire concept is still in the formative stage, and that much remains to be done before it will be practicable to use it operationally on a routine basis.

General characteristics of accuracy statistics

A basic characteristic of these "accuracy statistics" is that where conventional statistics are concerned with deviation of the examinee's score from the mean score, accuracy statistics are concerned with the deviation of his score from the mean *absolute* value on the underlying function measured by the test. (For instance in the case of the domain-referenced test of vocabulary that was discussed in Chapter 3, the underlying function would be the actual size of the examinee's recognition vocabulary.) Where conventional reliability statistics are concerned with the deviation of an examinee's test score on a test from his "true score" with respect to the group on which the reliability coefficient is based, there is a corresponding "coefficient of accuracy." This coefficient corresponds roughly to the conventional reliability coefficient, but is concerned with the deviation of the estimate of the examinee's vocabulary size yielded by the test from his actual vocabulary size (the latter not being a function of the test).

As for conventional statistics such as standard deviation and correlation coefficient, which involve deviations of a test score from the group mean on that same variable, corresponding to those statistics are "accuracy analogues." The latter are statistics in which the deviation of the examinee's test score from the group's mean score on that test is replaced by the deviation from the group's mean score on the *absolute scale* for the *underlying function*.

It turns out that for many, perhaps most, of the basic relationships among ordinary "conventional" statistics, the analogous formulas for the corresponding accuracy statistics are very similar. This is summarized in Appendix B, Table B-2. In this appendix the Greek letter lambda (λ) is used to represent the various accuracy analogues of conventional statistics. The letter lambda was chosen for this purpose because it corresponds to L (for "Location"). The symbol λ' is used instead of λ when the assumption has to be made that whatever systematic error there is in the absolute scores yielded by the test, it is uniform for all examinees. (Systematic error, in this sense, is defined as the deviation of the conventional "true score" on the test—in other words true score relative to the group—from the true *absolute* score). It should be noted that the assumption that systematic error is uniform at all parts of the score scale (i.e. the assumption made in the λ' modifications of the λ statistics) is not always a plausible one, and therefore should not be used except where necessary.

The accuracy statistic formulas generally reduce to the corresponding formulas for conventional statistics, when the assumption is made that there is no systematic error of measurement, only random error.

Coefficient of accuracy
Comparison with reliability coefficients

The coefficient of accuracy (λ_{ii}) was defined in the section above. Several formulas for it are given in Appendix B. (Formulas 11 b, 15, and 20 are for λ_{ii}. Formula 28 is for the modified coefficient, λ_{ii}'.)

Table 6-2 shows how reliability coefficients compare with coefficients of accuracy under various conditions, and how the λ accuracy coefficients compare with the λ' modifications. It will be noted that in the general situation the coefficient of accuracy is lower than the reliability coefficient. This is to be expected since, unlike the reliability coefficient, the coefficient of accuracy is affected not only by random error but also by systematic error.

Comparison with Livingston's "reliability coefficient"

It should be noted that the coefficient of accuracy is somewhat similar to Livingston's formula (discussed above). There is only one difference between the two formulas, but it is a crucial one. Where the coefficient of accuracy uses the true absolute score (i.e. the absolute score on the underlying function measured by the test) the Livingston coefficient uses the "criterion score" (i.e. the cutting score). The problems in connection with the Livingston coefficient were mentioned in the section above. The coefficient of accuracy is free of those problems, and yet it has all the advantages Livingston cites for his statistic.

The following formula shows the relationship of Livingston's coefficient (ρ) to the coefficients of reliability (r) and accuracy (λ).

$$1 \geq \rho_{aa} \geq r_{aa} \geq \lambda \geq \lambda'_{aa} \geq 0$$

Table 6-2. Reliability Coefficients and Coefficients of Accuracy for Specified Combinations of Random Error and Systematic Error.

Systematic error (δ) ↓ / Random error (ϵ) →	$\dfrac{\sigma_\epsilon^2}{\sigma_a^2} = 0$	$1 > \dfrac{\sigma_\epsilon^2}{\sigma_a^2} > 0$	$\dfrac{\sigma_\epsilon^2}{\sigma_a^2} = 1$
$\sigma_\delta = 0 \quad \bar{\delta} = 0$	$r_{ii} = \lambda_{ii} = 1$	$1 > r_{ii} = \lambda_{ii} > 0$	$r_{ii} = \lambda_{ii} = 0$
$\sigma_\delta = 0 \quad \bar{\delta} \neq 0$	$r_{ii} = 1$ $1 > \lambda_{ii}' = \lambda_{ii} > 0$	$1 > r_{ii} > \lambda_{ii}' = \lambda_{ii} > 0$	$r_{ii} = \lambda_{ii} = 0$
$\sigma_\delta \neq 0$	$r_{ii} = 1$ $1 > \lambda_{ii}' > \lambda_{ii} > 0$	$1 > r_{ii} > \lambda_{ii}' > \lambda_{ii} > 0$	

NOTES: Notation is as shown in Appendix B.

When σ_ϵ is computed at a specific score level rather than overall, it is mathematically possible (though unlikely) that $\sigma_\epsilon > \sigma_i$. In this event, assume $\sigma_\epsilon = \sigma_i$ in order to avoid negative reliability and accuracy, which are conceptually illogical.

Evaluation of the usefulness of the coefficient of accuracy (and the other accuracy statistics)

Standard statistical formulas involving or applicable to reliability coefficients are also applicable in terms of the corresponding accuracy statistics. For instance the formulas for correcting correlation coefficients for range and for attenuation have accuracy statistic analogues.

The principal problem in connection with the coefficient of accuracy and the other accuracy statistics is that to compute them requires information that is generally not available (i.e. information about the magnitude of systematic error). As a matter of fact, if we could find out that information accurately, we would not need a coefficient of accuracy to tell us how much the measurements provided by the test are impaired by those systematic errors. Knowing them, we could correct for them, thus solving the problem in the best possible way—by eliminating it.

Nevertheless the coefficient of accuracy and the other accuracy statistics do seem to have some real advantages of a conceptual nature, for use in connection with criterion-referenced tests. It may be worth while to compute the accuracy statistics making various assumptions about the magnitude of systematic errors. This might be helpful in providing a better understanding of how effective a particular criterion-referenced test seems to be. As has already been suggested, however, a lot more developmental work on these and related formulas needs to be done before accuracy statistics can become an effective operational part of the test evaluator's tool kit.

NOTES

[1] The term "coefficient of accuracy" is defined and discussed later in this chapter. It is a new psychometric statistic, applicable primarily to criterion-referenced tests.

[2] The variable of interest can also be the residual posttest score after pretest score has been covaried out; or one of the other variants proposed by Horst, Tallmadge, and Wood (1974).

[3] See, for instance, the quotation from Popham and Husek (1969) at the beginning of this chapter.

[4] It is quite similar to the one proposed in this book; they appear to have been developed independently and concurrently.

Evaluating criterion-referenced tests

[5] For further discussion of issues involved in choice of type of reliability coefficient, see Shaycoft, 1967, Chapter 4, pp. 4-9 through 4-15. (Also see the next subsection of this chapter.)

[6] More complicated procedures, not described here, would involve efforts to split out the vertical (interoccasion) and horizontal (interindividual) components of reliability.

7

Summary

It has become fashionable in recent years to classify achievement tests as norm-referenced or criterion-referenced, to imply that the latter should supplant the former, and to state that psychometric concepts such as validity and reliability, allegedly developed specifically for norm-referenced tests, are inappropriate in connection with criterion-referenced tests.

The writer of this book shares much of the enthusiasm about criterion-referenced tests, but also shares with the critics and doubters a substantial amount of skepticism, and a feeling that many of the claims have been overblown and are based on uncritical acceptance of ideas founded in misconceptions.

The title of this book indicates its main focus, criterion-referenced tests. But in focusing on criterion-referenced tests, this book inevitably has provided at least a peripheral view of norm-referenced tests, because the viewpoint throughout has been that there are fewer differences and more similarities between "norm-referenced" and criterion-referenced" tests than is usually supposed. As a matter of fact an entire chapter is devoted to the topic of norms for criterion-referenced tests. It is only a short chapter, because norms for criterion-referenced tests are really not different in any essential way from norms for other tests. But the important point is that either explicitly or implicitly (usually the latter), norms of some sort (or at least a normative concept) underlie every criterion-referenced test. These underlying norms may be vague, informal, rudimentary, and even, unfortunately, badly inaccurate, but somehow, in some way, they are there.

Throughout this book, in comparing criterion-referenced tests with other tests, we have in many places avoided calling those other tests "norm-referenced"; instead, we have referred to them as "tests that are not criterion-referenced." We have used this somewhat wordy locution in the hopes of reminding the reader that criterion-referenced tests are merely a special category of norm-

Summary

referenced tests, not a separate species.

As a matter of fact, if we had been willing to be even wordier, we could have been still more precise by avoiding the term "criterion-referenced test" too. Actually there is no such thing as a "criterion-referenced test"; that term is really just a kind of shorthand for "a test for which a criterion-referenced interpretation is given to the scores."

SCOPE AND CONTENT

This book is concerned almost exclusively with paper-and-pencil criterion-referenced tests rather than performance tests. The focus is primarily on the use of tests in educational measurement.

One way of viewing much of the contents is as being divided into two major aspects: (1) what some readers may regard as an iconoclastic approach to what the author regards as popular misconceptions about criterion-referenced tests (see "Shattered Icons" below), and (2) what are hoped to be constructive suggestions about how to develop, use, and evaluate criterion-referenced tests (see "Suggestions on Approaches and Procedures" below).

DEFINITIONS OF BASIC TERMS

Criterion-referenced tests

In criterion-referenced measurements—unlike norm-referenced measurement—scores are interpreted as having some sort of absolute meaning in terms, for instance, of level of performance or amount achieved or degree of mastery. In other words the criterion-referenced score has some sort of meaning in itself, irrespective of the scores for specified groups. (Although the term "criterion-referenced tests" was not coined until 1963, the concept had been in existence for a long time before that.)

Kinds of criterion-referenced tests

A distinction is made between two basic kinds of criterion-referenced measurement: domain-referenced and objective-referenced.

Domain-referenced measurement

In a domain-referenced test the overall score has absolute meaning (criterion-referenced meaning) in the sense of indicating what proportion of some defined domain the examinee has mastered. This type of measurement is most suitable when the area to be measured is a domain that can be clearly defined, and from which a probability sample can be drawn.

Objective-referenced measurement

Objective-referenced measurement refers to the kind of test (or subtest) that corresponds to a specific objective of instruction or a specific objective that is to be achieved by the examinee. The test or subtest usually consists of a comparatively small number of items drawn from a larger set of possible items. Scores on an objective-referenced test are usually dichotomized by a cutting score; examinees with scores at or above the cutting score are deemed to have met the objective.

Behavioral objectives

These are sometimes defined as objectives couched in such terms that they indicate what the individual is *doing* that is *observable* (in other words, how he is behaving) when he is demonstrating that he has met the behavioral objective. (This definition rules out such constructs as "understanding," "appreciating," and "feeling," since they are not exactly visible to the observer.)

SHATTERED ICONS
(A NEW KIND OF TABLE OF CONTENTS)

Because the attempted demolition of misconceptions constitutes such a large part of this book and because this material is scattered through all chapters, some readers might find it convenient to have a sort of table of contents built around these "shattered icons". Table 7-1 does just that. It lists the misconceptions (fallacies) briefly and tells on what pages they are discussed.

Table 7-1. Summary of Prevalent Fallacies Discussed in This Book.

Topic		Fallacy		Fact	Pages
A. Relation between criterion-referenced and norm-referenced tests	1.	That there are two kinds of tests: norm-referenced and criterion-referenced. A test is one or the other—not both.	1a.	Some tests are both norm-referenced and criterion-referenced.	1, 11–13, 16, 56, 59–60, 100–101
			1b.	Some tests are neither.	9–11
	2a.	That criterion-referenced tests are innately superior to norm-referenced tests.	2.	Insofar as there is a real distinction it is in purpose and uses. Each has appropriate functions, and both categories of test are useful.	1, 100–101
	2b.	That criterion-referenced tests should be substituted for norm-referenced tests in all contexts where the latter are now commonly used.			
B. Norm-referenced tests	1.	That when the final form of a norm-refer-	1.	In constructing an achievement test prop-	51–53

(continued)

Table 7-1 (continued)

Topic	Fallacy	Fact	Pages
B. Norm-referenced tests (continued)	erly, considerable attention is being developed, items are selected for it solely on the basis of item statistics; no attention is paid to content distribution.	attention is paid to content distribution.	
	2. That the ideal norm-referenced test would consist of items with difficulty coefficients (proportion of the group knowing the answer) as close to .50 as possible.	2. Item difficulties in the ideal achievement test are spread over a wide range.	52
	3. That in picking items for a norm-referenced test it is customary to select the items that have the highest coefficients of internal consistency—in other	3. Coefficients of internal consistency are used primarily to eliminate unsatisfactory items—not to identify the "best" items.	52–53

		words the most discriminating items.		
	4.	That grade equivalents are the most useful and meaningful kind of norm.	4.	For most tests grade equivalents give a spurious appearance of meaningfulness. Actually they are misleading and should seldom, if ever, be used.	57–58, 113
C. Criterion-referenced tests	1.	That "classical" psychometric theory is inapplicable to criterion-referenced tests.	1.	Classical psychometric theory is entirely applicable. Those who think it is not may misunderstand classical psychometric theory.	1, 52, 80–94, 115–116
	1a.	That the concept of "reliability," in particular, is inapplicable.			1, 86–91, 115–116
	1b.	That criterion-referenced tests are not at all like norm-referenced tests in terms of desirable item characteristics.			51–53, 113

(continued)

Table 7-1 (continued)

Topic		Fallacy		Fact	Pages
C. Criterion-referenced tests (continued)	2.	That in developing a criterion-referenced test the goal necessarily should be a test on which everyone in the group performs perfectly, or nearly perfectly.	2.	The objective of *instruction* should be mastery learning, but the goal of the test is just to *describe* the degree of success with which that objective is reached—not to guarantee that the objective is reached.	80–83
	3.	That criterion-referenced tests do not have and do not need norms.	3.	Many of these tests have norms, and all of them need them—at least as a basis for planning, and at least on an informal basis.	1, 56
	4.	That criterion-referenced tests were invented in the 1960s.	4.	They existed a long time before that. Only the name was new.	5–8
	5.	That criterion-referenced tests ideally	5.	Items should *not* be thrown out merely be-	1, 53–54

	should consist of items that everyone can answer correctly.	cause, even in a post-test situation, they fail to show close to 100% correct.	
6.	That objective-referenced tests require a cutting score that differentiates in some absolute way between satisfactory and unsatisfactory.	6. Even in the case of objective-referenced tests, it is better to use a continuous scale than a dichotomous scale in scoring, since the continuous scale provides more information.	13–15
7.	The cutting score (the percentage of the items the examinee must answer correctly to pass) is a value that distinguishes in some absolute way between those who have mastered the objective and those who have not; it has nothing to do with norms.	7. The standards that are set have to be determined not only by what is desirable but by what can realistically be expected.	67–70

(continued)

Table 7-1 (continued)

Topic		Fallacy		Fact	Pages
C. Criterion-referenced tests (continued)	8.	That if the cutting score on an objective-referenced test is 85% right (or any other specified percentage) that number represents the *percentage of the entire domain* that the examinee has mastered.	8.	The lower the performance level of the group, the higher the cutting score has to be set in order to minimize misclassification as to whether a given percentage of the entire domain has been mastered.	67, 70–71, 114
	9.	That the proportion of items answered correctly in a multiple-choice test represents proportion mastered.	9.	Some sort of correction for chance is necessary, if the proportion is to have any sort of absolute meaning.	59, 76–79
	10.	That one form of a criterion-referenced test is enough, since the test *is* the criterion.	10.	Multiple forms are needed for any cognitive test that covers merely a *sample* of the domain, if there is to be retesting.	72–74, 112, 114

D. Predictive tests	1.	That "predictive tests" (tests intended to predict performance at some future time as indicated by an appropriate criterion measure) should be "criterion-referenced" in the sense in which that term is commonly used (in this book and elsewhere).	9–10, 16
	1a.	An achievement test, whether norm-referenced or criterion-referenced, can also be used for predictive purposes.	
	1b.	The concept of criterion-referenced measurement is seldom, if ever, applicable to predictive uses of tests.	1, 10–11, 16, 93–94
E. Behavioral objectives	1.	That defining an instructional program entirely in terms of behavioral objectives is a panacea.	
	1.	Many so-called behavioral objectives are merely test items—so that in effect the test is determining the objectives and the program, not vice versa.	22–26, 111–112, 113–114
	2.	That behavioral objectives of instruction in the sense in which the term is usually used, to define test items, are *the* objectives.	
	2.	The ultimate objectives are more important (though less measurable) than the immediate "behavioral objectives."	26–28, 111–112, 113–114

(continued)

Table 7-1 (continued)

Topic	Fallacy	Fact	Pages
F. Multiple-choice tests in general	1. That the only situation in which there is any value in correcting scores for chance is when the test is speeded.	1. Correcting for chance is important any time examinees differ in their tendency to guess rather than omit items (as well as when they differ in the number of items they do not have time to respond to).	59, 76–79, 115

SUGGESTIONS ON APPROACHES AND PROCEDURES

Developing criterion-referenced tests

If one is convinced that he needs a criterion-referenced test for research purposes or for operational use in schools, he is up against the problem of how to construct such a test (or alternatively, how to select one from among those commercially available). The literature is replete with advice to base criterion-referenced tests on behavioral objectives and with explanations of what behavioral objectives are (Mager, 1961; Mager, 1962; Mager, 1972; Dillman, 1971; Popham and Baker, 1970; Gronlund, 1970; Geis, 1972). But there seems to be little or nothing in print that explains clearly what relationship there should be between the behavioral objective and the test item, how one gets from one to the other, and how one avoids the teaching-to-the-test pitfall. This is a very tricky problem, not nearly as simple as it seems. It has four aspects: (1) establishing appropriate objectives, with the right degree of immediacy and the right degree of specificity; (2) figuring out how to get from the objectives to the test itself—in other words what kind of test will measure what one wants to measure; (3) selecting the sample of domain elements to be covered by the test; and (4) actually writing the test in accordance with the plan.

Objectives

The concept of "behavioral objectives" has acquired considerable popularity in recent years. It is useful provided that the objectives are appropriate ones, rather than having been adopted merely because they are easy to put in behavioral terms, which all too often are nothing more than a set of test items together with suggested cutting scores. This whole problem is discussed in Chapter 3, in the section "Defining What Is to Be Measured," where attention is also drawn to the importance of ultimate objectives; these, unfortunately, are often ignored in the mad rush toward the more immediate "behavioral objectives."

Test rationales

The use of test rationales (Flanagan, 1951a) is recommended to provide the linkage between the objectives and the test. That concept needs to be incorporated into the "behavioral objectives" routine, in order to prevent what otherwise occurs all too frequently—the merger of behavioral objective and test specification into one blurry, overextended conglomerate. Test rationales are discussed in Chapter 3.

Sampling the domain

In the case of domain-referenced tests a formal sampling procedure is usually necessary to select the specific content to be included in the test. This is important because a genuine probability sample of the domain is needed if the test scores are to have "absolute meaning." In the opinion of the author of this book, however, for objective-referenced tests formal sampling is seldom essential.

It is essential that parallel forms be available if a test is to be administered more than once to the same examinee. In constructing parallel forms, it is essential to have an independent sampling of content for each form, instead of making the forms excessively similar by using essentially the same content sample and merely altering each item slightly to create a "new" form. Domain sampling is discussed in Chapter 3, in the section on "Sampling from the Domain."

Writing the items

The importance of this aspect of test development is stressed. Efforts to routinize it (through the use of "item shells" and through construction by computer) typically result in degradation of test quality (e.g. substantially lowered reliability). The importance of having test development (including item writing) done by experts is stressed.

Planning the nature of the test items is an integral part of the test rationale. This aspect, including numerous examples of good and bad items, is discussed in Chapter 3, in the section on "Writing the Test Items."

Tryout and item analysis

This is discussed in the Chapter 3 section "Tryout and Item Analysis." It is pointed out that for some tests of the domain-referenced type, item analysis may not be necessary; it may, in fact, be quite superfluous. For objective-referenced tests, amount of time in the course, extending from none at all (pretest) to completion (posttest), is a useful criterion.

Norms for criterion-referenced tests

Percentile norms are vastly superior to norms of the grade-equivalent type. The latter have so many disadvantages and they result in so much misinterpretation, misunderstanding, and misuse that complete abandonment of the concept could result in a net gain. This is discussed in Chapter 4.

Using criterion-referenced tests

Before one decides to use a criterion-referenced approach in developing a test it is important that he *think through* the implications of the test's proposed functions and make certain that criterion-referencing is a valid way of fulfilling those functions.

Relation between what is tested, what is taught, and what the objectives are

1. It is imperative that "teaching to the test" be avoided. One of the problems with using objective-referenced tests is that they produce a strong temptation to teach to the test; teachers and adminis-

trators should be aware of the problem and take steps to prevent it. *The test must not determine what is taught.*

2. Conversely, *what is taught should not determine what is tested,* if one is trying to determine how well the objectives have been met.

3. The objectives should determine the test content.

4. The objectives should also determine what is taught, and how.

Cutting scores and standards of competence

In using criterion-referenced tests, particularly those of the objective-referenced type, a distinction has to be drawn between the "standard of competence" and the cutting score; the former applies to the domain as a whole—the universe of potential test items—while the latter applies only to the specific test.

Likewise a parallel distinction must be drawn between the examinee's level of competence on the domain as a whole and his test score. It is shown (in Appendix A) that when reduced to percentage scores, these two values for the examinee may differ systematically. This has to be taken into account in setting the cutting score, if misclassifications are to be minimized. It turns out that the more competent the group as a whole, the *lower* the cutting score may be set. Thus if a pretest is being given to determine which examinees have achieved a sufficiently high level of competence to be exempted from a particular course, the cutting score should be set higher than it is for the posttest administered upon completion of the course.

Repeated testings

In most situations in which repeated testings are called for, different forms of the test must be used on each occasion. There are only two exceptions to this rule:

1. When the test is one for which memorization cannot be a factor and practice effect is either nonexistent or negligible.

2. When the test is identical with the domain—in other words when the test items are not merely a small sample of the items that constitute the domain, but instead are a 100% sample.

Summary

Scoring multiple-choice criterion-referenced tests

Correcting multiple-choice scores for chance is a good general practice, because it improves the validity of the scores. But it is *especially* important for criterion-referenced tests, because only if the correction is made is there any basis for assuming that the percentage score is a reasonable estimate of percentage of the domain mastered (i.e. percentage of the domain of items *to which the answer is known,* as opposed to the somewhat larger percentage answered correctly). If scores are not corrected for chance there is no sensible way of generalizing from score to domain; this completely invalidates the criterion-referencing feature of the test—that is, the meaningful absolute scores.

Evaluating criterion-referenced tests

Contrary to what many writers have asserted, the full range of standard psychometric procedures applies to criterion-referenced tests, since, as has already been pointed out, they are essentially a special kind of norm-referenced test. (But *since* they are a special kind, they may require some *special* statistical procedures in addition to the standard ones applicable to tests in general. See "Accuracy Statistics" below.)

Reliability

Suggested procedures

1. *For objective-referenced tests:* Most of the main uses of objective-referenced tests involve a comparison between pretest and posttest scores, and an expectation that there will be a difference between them. Therefore the set of scores with which we should be concerned in determining the reliability of a criterion-referenced test is the full range of scores extending from those who have had no instruction in a unit or module corresponding to the objectives measured to those who have presumably completed the instructional program. Procedures are described in the first section of Chapter 6 for obtaining reliability coefficients using such data.

2. *For domain-referenced tests:* For domain-referenced tests to be used for the evaluation of individuals, direct computation of parallel-forms reliability is recommended. Split-half reliability is also a possibility if the nature of the test is such that it does not rule this out.

Comments on the Livingston procedure. This procedure (Livingston, 1970, 1972) produces a statistic that is called a reliability coefficient, but really is not and should not be used for that purpose. (This is discussed in the first section of Chapter 6.)

Validation of criterion-referenced tests

For evaluating the achievement of individuals or groups. Appropriate external criteria seldom exist for achievement tests, whether criterion-referenced or not. Content validation is the only kind usually feasible. Fortunately careful and skilled test construction, in conjunction with predetermined and very detailed test objectives, can usually establish the content validity of a test even though an adequate external criterion is not available. (See the Chapter 6 section "Validity.")

For evaluating the effectiveness of an educational program. One approach to this problem is to validate the test score against time elapsed since the beginning of the course, or percentage of the course completed. (See Chapter 6, "Validity.")

"Accuracy statistics"

Conventional psychometric statistics (reliability and validity coefficients, etc.) give no information whatever concerning the accuracy of the absolute numbers that are supposed to indicate (in absolute terms) degree of mastery of the domain. Therefore it would be desirable to have, in addition to the conventional statistics, some special statistics that give the extra information that is relevant for criterion-referenced tests. A beginning has been made, in Appendix B, toward deriving just such a set of statistics. They are discussed briefly in Chapter 6, in the section on "Accuracy."

One of the new statistics is called a "coefficient of accuracy." It is in some ways analogous to a reliability coefficient, though it is systematically lower, because it is reduced by systematic errors of measurement as well as by random errors of measurement.

Although these new statistics are difficult to compute (and as a matter of fact some of them are at present impossible to compute), nevertheless they do seem to have some real advantages of a conceptual nature, for use with criterion-referenced tests. But a lot more developmental work needs to be done on them.

A FINAL WORD

As was implied at the beginning of this book and has been alluded to at various points throughout, the large body of literature about criterion-referenced tests that exists by now includes a vast stock of nonsense. The author of this book hopes sincerely that she has not added to the stock.

References

Angoff, W. H. Test reliability and effective test length. *Psychometrika*, 1953, *18*, 1-14.

Angoff, W. H. Criterion-referencing, norm-referencing, and the SAT. *College Board Review*, 1974, *92*, 2-5.

Carver, R. P. Two dimensions of tests: Psychometric and edumetric. *American Psychologist*, 1974, *29*, 512-518. (Note: Comments on this article appeared in the *American Psychologist*, 1975, *30:* King, D. J., page 602; Cronbach, L. J., pages 602-3; Haladyna, T. M., pages 603-4; Gladstone, R., pages 604-5.)

Davis, F. B. A note on the correction for chance success. *Journal of Experimental Education*, Spring 1967, *35*(3), 42-47.

Davis, F. B., and Diamond, J. J. The preparation of criterion-referenced tests. *CSE Monograph Series in Evaluation, #3: Problems in criterion-referenced measurement*, 1974, 116-138.

Dillman, F. E., Jr. *Instructional objectives; Specificity and behavior.* Menlo Park, Calif.: Dillman Associates, 1971.

Ebel, R. L. Content standard test scores. *Educational and Psychological Measurement*, 1962, *22*, 15-25.

Ebel, R. L. Knowledge vs. ability in achievement testing. *Invitational Conference on Testing Problems*. Princeton, N.J.: Educational Testing Service, 1969, 66-76.

Ebel, R. L. Some limitations of criterion-referenced measurement. Paper presented at the meeting of the American Educational Research Association, Minneapolis, March 1970.

Ebel, R. L. Evaluation and Educational objectives. *Journal of Educational Measurement*, 1973, *10*, 273-279.

Flanagan, J. C. *Cooperative achievement tests: A bulletin reporting the basic principles and procedures used in the development of their system of scaled scores.* New York: Cooperative Test Service, December 1939.

Flanagan, J. C. The use of comprehensive rationales in test development. *Educational and Psychological Measurement*, 1951a, *11*, 151-155.

References

Flanagan, J. C. Units, scores, and norms. In E. F. Lindquist (Ed.), *Educational measurement*. Washington, D.C.: American Council on Education, 1951b, pages 695-763.

Geis, G. L. *Behavioral objectives. A selected bibliography and brief review*. Montreal: Centre for Learning and Development, McGill University, 1972.

Glaser, R. Instructional technology and the measurement of learning outcomes. *American Psychologist*, 1963, *18*, 518-521.

Gronlund, N. E. *Stating behavioral objectives for classroom instruction*. Toronto: The Macmillan Co., Collier-Macmillan Canada, Lt., 1970.

Hively, W. AERA Symposium: Domain-referenced achievement testing. February, 1970.

Hively, W., Patterson, H. L., and Page, S. A "universe-defined" system of arithmetic achievement tests. *Journal of Educational Measurement*, 1968, *5*, 275-290.

Horst, D. P., Tallmadge, G. K., and Wood, C. T. Measuring achievement gains in educational projects. Los Altos, Calif.: RMC Research Corporation, 1974.

Kelley, T. L. *Fundamentals of statistics*. Cambridge, Mass.: Harvard University Press, 1947.

Kuder, G. F., and Richardson, M. W. The theory of test reliability. *Psychometrika*, 1937, *2*, 151-160.

Lindquist, E. F. Preliminary considerations in objective test construction. In E. F. Lindquist (Ed.), *Educational measurement*. Washington, D.C.: American Council on Education, 1951, pages 119-158.

Livingston, S. A. *The reliability of criterion-referenced measures*. Baltimore: Johns Hopkins University, Center for the Study of Social Organization of Schools, Report #0.73, 1970.

Livingston, S. A. Criterion-referenced applications of classical test theory. *Journal of Educational Measurement*, Spring 1972, *9*(1), 13-29.

Lorge, I., and Chall, J. Estimating the size of vocabularies of children and adults: An analysis of methodological issues. *Journal of Experimental Education*, Winter 1963, *32*(2), 147-157.

Mager, R. F. *Preparing objectives for programmed instruction*. San Francisco: Fearon Publishers, 1961.

Mager, R. F. *Preparing instructional objectives*. Palo Alto, Calif.: Fearon Publishers, 1962.

Mager, R. F. *Developing attitude toward learning*. Palo Alto, Calif.: Fearon Publishers, 1968.

Mager, R. F. *Goal analysis*. Belmont, Calif.: Fearon Publishers/Lear Siegler, Inc., Educational Division, 1972.

Mattson, D. E. Criterion related measures in education—an appealing delusion. Paper presented at the meeting of the American Educational Research Association, Minneapolis, March 1970.

Meskauskas, J. A. Evaluation models for criterion-referenced testing: Views regarding mastery and standard-setting. *Review of Educational Research,* 1976, *46,* 133–158.

Millman, J. Passing scores and test lengths for domain-referenced measures. *Review of Educational Research,* 1973, *43,* 205–216.

Nitko, A. J. Some considerations when using a domain-referenced system of achievement tests in instructional situations. Paper presented at the meeting of the American Educational Research Association, Minneapolis, March 1970.

Popham, W. J. Selecting objectives and generating test items for objective-based tests. *CSE Monograph Series in Evaluation, #3: Problems in criterion-referenced measurement,* 1974, 13–25.

Popham, W. J. *Evaluation in education: Current applications.* Berkeley, Calif.: McCutchan Publishing Co., 1974.

Popham, W. J., and Baker, E. L. *Establishing instructional goals.* Englewood Cliffs, N.J.: Prentice-Hall, 1970.

Popham, W. J., and Husek, T. R. Implications of criterion-referenced measurement. *Journal of Educational Measurement,* 1969, *6,* 1–9.

Richards, J. M., Jr. Can computers write college admissions tests? *Journal of Applied Psychology,* 1957, *51,* 211–215.

Shaycoft, M. F. Chapter 3 in Flanagan, J. C., Davis, F. B., Dailey, J. T., Shaycoft, Marion F., Orr, D. B., Goldberg, I., and Neyman, C. A., Jr. *The American high school student.* (Final report to the U.S. Office of Education, Cooperative Research Project No. 635.) Washington, D.C.: Univer. of Pittsburgh, Project TALENT Office, 1964.

Shaycoft, M. F. *The high school years: Growth in cognitive skills.* (Interim report 3 to the U.S. Office of Education, Cooperative Research Project No. 3051.) Pittsburgh: American Institutes for Research and Univer. of Pittsburgh, Project TALENT Office, 1967.

Shaycoft, M. F. Development and analysis of a test to estimate size of vocabulary. (Paper presented at American Psychological Association convention, in Chicago, 9/7/65, revised 2/26/68.) Palo Alto: American Institutes for Research, 1968.

Tallmadge, G. K., and Horst, D. P. A procedural guide for validating achievement gains in educational projects. Los Altos, Calif.: RMC Research Corporation, 1974.

Thorndike, E. L., and Lorge, I. *The teacher's word book of 30,000 words.* New York: Bureau of Publications, Teachers College, Columbia University, 1944.

Thorndike, E. L. The vocabularies of school pupils. *Contributions to Education*, I (New York: The World Book Company, 1924), 69–76.

Warrington, W. G. Criterion related measures: Some general considerations. Paper presented at the meeting of the American Educational Research Association, Minneapolis, March 1970.

Wight, A. R. Beyond behavioral objectives. *Educational Technology*, July 1972, 9–14.

APPENDIX A.
A paradox in setting cutting scores on criterion-referenced tests[1]

THE PROBLEM

For each examinee on a criterion-referenced test there is a competence level (percentage of all possible items in the domain to which he knows the answer) and a score (percentage of test items he answers correctly, in a random sample of all possible items). Corresponding to these, if the criterion-referenced test is of the type sometimes called objective-referenced, a standard of competence that examinees are to meet and a cutting score on the test are set. This appendix is concerned with how and where the cutting score should be set. First, however, let us consider the standard of competence.

Let us assume that a standard of competence (or of achievement, or accomplishment) has been set for some "domain" of knowledge—perhaps arbitrarily or perhaps on an informed basis. For instance suppose the standard is set at 80%. That means that if there is good reason to believe a person has mastered 80% of the *entire* domain (not just 80% of that sample of the domain that was included in the criterion-referenced test), he will be certified to have achieved the established standard of mastery, or to have passed the examination; and that therefore, in view of this accomplishment, he will be entitled to all the perquisites pertaining thereunto. What those perquisites are will depend on the nature of the domain, the kind of person to whom the examination applies, and other characteristics of the situation. For instance for an elementary-school student in some kind of individualized instruction program, the test may be designed to determine whether he has mastered a particular module or unit of instruction and may therefore proceed to the next one. Or a set of examinations may be used for course placement of a student—for instance to determine whether a student who has studied analytic geometry by himself and has had no formal instruction in it has mastered the concepts he will need in calculus well enough to be permitted to skip the analytic geometry course and go directly into a calculus course.

Whatever the situation, a cutting point must be set on the test. In this connection, the following questions must be answered:

1. Should the cutting point on the test correspond exactly to the standard set for mastery of the entire domain? For instance, if it has been decided that mastery of 80% of the *domain* is needed, should the passing mark on the criterion-referenced test be set at 80% correct?

2. If not, should the cutting point be set at the same level for everybody? More specifically, should it be the same for the student who has not taken the course (or studied the module) and wishes to be exempted from it as for the student who has completed the course?

3. If the cutting point is not to be set to correspond exactly to the established standard of mastery, where should it be set, and why?

PERSPECTIVE AND THEORETICAL FRAMEWORK

Errors of measurement in criterion-referenced tests

In criterion-referenced measurement, unlike norm-referenced measurement, the purpose is to determine whether the examinee has met some absolute standard rather than a standard expressed in terms of how he compares with his fellow examinees. But this cannot be accomplished perfectly, not only because every test has some random error of measurement, but also because in the case of criterion-referenced measurement the definition of "error of measurement" should be expanded to include a systematic error component as well. If the standard of competence has been set at 80% one does not want someone to be considered to have achieved that standard if he has not (nor to be considered *not* to have met the standard if in actuality he has) no matter how high (or low) he has scored in comparison with his peers. In terms of "classical" psychometric concepts the whole score scale might be displaced upward or downward by a constant amount without affecting the conventional coefficient of reliability at all, and without affecting error of measurement, as conventionally defined. But displacement of the score scale adds a systematic error to the usual random measurement errors. Thus in considering whether the test score is likely to have classified an examinee properly, it is necessary to consider how that test score is likely to compare not merely with the cutting score but also with the established standard of competence.

Mathematical model

The binomial distribution provides the basic mathematical model. For a test whose items are completion type or some other type that requires the examinee to *construct* the answer rather than merely to *select* it from among two or more choices provided, it is assumed that for examinees who have mastered any specified proportion (P) of the potential test items in the entire domain, the distribution of scores on the n-item test will be binomial. It should be borne in mind that this statement applies to a segment of the total population that is homogeneous with respect to proportion of the domain mastered. A matrix of these binomial distributions, with a different row for each P value, may be developed. This is matrix **K** (K for "known"). All notation is explained in Exhibit A-1 and a sample of the matrix is shown in Table A-1.

Furthermore, in the case of multiple-choice tests, it is assumed that another binomial distribution governs the probability that an individual will *guess* a specified number of items *correctly,* from among all those to which he does not *know* the answer. The items whose answers he does not know are assumed to be identical in content tested to the ones he would be unable to respond to correctly if the test were of the constructed-answer type.

A matrix of these binomial distributions of number of items guessed incorrectly may also be developed. This is matrix **W** (W for "wrong"). The binomial distributions constituting matrix **W** are based on the assumption that, to the extent that one does not know the answer, pure guessing operates; systematic misinformation is ruled out.

Exhibit A-1. Notation and Formulas

Notation

- n = no. of items in test constituting a hypothetical random sample of the domain
- c = no. of options per item
- P = competence level, expressed as a proportion of the domain mastered
- L = no. of competence levels for which tables are to be computed
- p = probability value used for binominal distribution

Matrices

Matrix **K**

L rows, each corresponding to a value of P

$n + 1$ columns, running from 0 to n, each corresponding to a score on a constructed-answer test

Each element of the matrix is the theoretical proportion of cases in the row knowing the answers to a specified number of items in a constructed-answer test consisting of n items which are a random sample of the domain.

Each row is an n-element binomial distribution for which

$$p = P \qquad (1)$$

Matrix **W**

$n + 1$ rows, running from 0 to n, each row corresponding to number of test items to which answer is *known*

$n + 1$ columns, running from n to 0, each column corresponding to number of items *guessed incorrectly*

Each element of the matrix is the theoretical proportion of cases in the row *guessing incorrectly* the specified number of items.

Each row is an n-element binomial distibution for which

$$p = \frac{1}{c} \qquad (2)$$

This is the probability of getting the item right by chance, if one has no idea of the answer.

Matrix **X**

L rows, each corresponding to a value of P

$n + 1$ columns, running from 0 to n, each column corresponding to the raw score (no. of correct answers)

(continued)

Exhibit A-1 (continued)

Matrices
 Matrix **X**

> Each element of the matrix is the theoretical proportion of the row's cases having the specified score on the n-item multiple-choice test.
>
> Matrix multiplication formula for matrix **X**:
>
> $$\mathbf{X} = \mathbf{KW} \qquad (3)$$

Matrix **K** and matrix **W** are then multiplied to yield matrix **X**, each row of which is a hypothetical score distribution for individuals at a specified level of competence in the domain from which the test items are a sample. Table A-1, which shows a **K** matrix in the lower left corner for a five-item test, also shows the corresponding **W** and **X** matrices for a five-item multiple-choice test with four choices per item.

Table A-2a presents matrix **K** data, in a slightly modified format, for constructed-answer tests. Tables A-2b, A-2c, A-2d, and A-2e present matrix **X** data (the hypothetical multiple-choice score distributions) in the same modified format, for five-choice, four-choice, three-choice, and two-choice items respectively.

Table A-3 shows the proportion of cases at various levels of competence who would pass and the proportion who would fail, if the cutting score (percent right) were set at various points (60%, 70%, 80%, 90%, 100%).

Table A-4 presents some hypothetical distributions of the competence level mix that might describe a group at different stages in the instructional program. The stage 1 column might be the preinstruction distribution while stage 5 might be near the end of the instructional program—at least for a sizable proportion of the group.

Table A-5 shows what percentage of students would be classified correctly and what percentage would be misclassified, using various cutting scores, at various stages. For this purpose two kinds of misclassification are recognized:

> 1. *False pass.* This occurs when an examinee whose competency level is *below* the standard that has been set scores *at or above* the cutting point.

(continued on p. 150)

Table A-1. Demonstration of Method of Calculating Theoretical Distribution of Scores (Matrix **X**)* on a Criterion-Referenced Test with a Specified Number of Items and a Specified Number of Options Per Item for Individuals at Specified Levels of Competence

Data for example
$n = 5$
$c = 4$
$L = 2$
$P = .80$
$P = .95$

		Matrix **W** No. guessed incorrectly					
		5	4	3	2	1	0
No. known	0	.237	.395	.264	.088	.015	.001
	1	.000	.316	.422	.211	.047	.004
	2	.000	.000	.422	.422	.141	.015
	3	.000	.000	.000	.563	.375	.062
	4	.000	.000	.000	.000	.750	.250
	5	.000	.000	.000	.000	.000	1.000

	Matrix **K** No. of answers known (constructed-answer test score)					
	0	1	2	3	4	5
$P = .80$	.000	.006	.051	.205	.410	.328
$P = .95$	.000	.000	.001	.021	.204	.774

	Matrix **X** No. of correct answers (multiple-choice test score)					
	0	1	2	3	4	5
$P = .80$	.000	.002	.024	.138	.392	.444
$P = .95$	.000	.000	.001	.012	.161	.826

*$\mathbf{X} = \mathbf{KW}$.

Table A-2a. Theoretical Distribution of Scores on Criterion-referenced Test Consisting of *Constructed-answer Items* (e.g. Completion Items) for Individuals at Specified Levels of Competence.

No. of items in test (n)	No. right (R)	% right	Percentage of cases												
			$P = .00$	$P = .01$	$P = .05$	$P = .10$	$P = .20$	$P = .30$	$P = .50$	$P = .70$	$P = .80$	$P = .90$	$P = .95$	$P = .99$	$P = 1.00$
5	5	100	.00	.00	.00	.00	.03	.24	3.13	16.81	32.77	59.06	77.39	95.10	100.00
	4	80	.00	.00	.00	.04	.64	2.83	15.63	36.02	40.96	32.80	20.36	4.80	.00
	3	60	.00	.00	.11	.81	5.12	13.23	31.24	30.87	20.48	7.29	2.14	.10	.00
	2	40	.00	.10	2.14	7.29	20.48	30.87	31.24	13.23	5.12	.81	.11	.00	.00
	1	20	.00	4.80	20.36	32.80	40.96	36.02	15.63	2.83	.64	.04	.00	.00	.00
	0	0	100.00	95.10	77.39	59.06	32.77	16.81	3.13	.24	.03	.00	.00	.00	.00
	Total		100.00	100.00	100.00	100.00	100.00	100.00	100.00	100.00	100.00	100.00	100.00	100.00	100.00
10	10	100	.00	.00	.00	.00	.00	.00	.10	2.82	10.74	34.87	59.87	90.43	100.00
	9	90	.00	.00	.00	.00	.00	.01	.98	12.11	26.84	38.74	31.51	9.14	.00
	8	80	.00	.00	.00	.00	.01	.14	4.39	23.35	30.20	19.37	7.46	.42	.00
	7	70	.00	.00	.00	.00	.08	.90	11.72	26.69	20.13	5.74	1.05	.01	.00
	6	60	.00	.00	.00	.01	.55	3.68	20.51	20.01	8.81	1.12	.10	.00	.00
	5	50	.00	.00	.01	.15	2.64	10.29	24.60	10.29	2.64	.15	.01	.00	.00
	4	40	.00	.00	.10	1.12	8.81	20.01	20.51	3.68	.55	.01	.00	.00	.00
	3	30	.00	.01	1.05	5.74	20.13	26.69	11.72	.90	.08	.00	.00	.00	.00
	2	20	.00	.42	7.46	19.37	30.20	23.35	4.39	.14	.01	.00	.00	.00	.00
	1	10	.00	9.14	31.51	38.74	26.84	12.11	.98	.01	.00	.00	.00	.00	.00
	0	0	100.00	90.43	59.87	34.87	10.74	2.82	.10	.00	.00	.00	.00	.00	.00
	Total		100.00	100.00	100.00	100.00	100.00	100.00	100.00	100.00	100.00	100.00	100.00	100.00	100.00

20	20	100	.00	.00	.00	.00	.00	.00	.00	.00	.08	1.15	12.16	35.85	81.79	100.00
	19	95	.00	.00	.00	.00	.00	.00	.02	.00	.68	5.76	27.01	37.74	16.52	.00
	18	90	.00	.00	.00	.00	.00	.00	.11	.00	2.78	13.69	28.51	18.87	1.59	.00
	17	85	.00	.00	.00	.00	.00	.00	.46	.02	7.16	20.54	19.01	5.96	.10	.00
	16	80	.00	.00	.00	.00	.00	.00	1.48	.11	13.04	21.82	8.98	1.33	.00	.00
	15	75	.00	.00	.00	.00	.00	.00	3.70	.46	17.89	17.46	3.19	.22	.00	.00
	14	70	.00	.00	.00	.00	.00	.02	7.39	1.48	19.17	10.91	.89	.03	.00	.00
	13	65	.00	.00	.00	.00	.00	.10	12.01	3.70	16.43	5.45	.20	.00	.00	.00
	12	60	.00	.00	.00	.00	.01	.39	16.02	7.39	11.44	2.22	.04	.00	.00	.00
	11	55	.00	.00	.00	.00	.05	1.20	17.62	12.01	6.54	.74	.01	.00	.00	.00
	10	50	.00	.00	.00	.00	.20	3.08	16.02	16.02	3.08	.20	.00	.00	.00	.00
	9	45	.00	.00	.00	.01	.74	6.54	12.01	17.62	1.20	.05	.00	.00	.00	.00
	8	40	.00	.00	.00	.04	2.22	11.44	7.39	16.02	.39	.01	.00	.00	.00	.00
	7	35	.00	.00	.00	.20	5.45	16.43	3.70	12.01	.10	.00	.00	.00	.00	.00
	6	30	.00	.00	.03	.89	10.91	19.17	1.48	7.39	.02	.00	.00	.00	.00	.00
	5	25	.00	.00	.22	3.19	17.46	17.89	.46	3.70	.00	.00	.00	.00	.00	.00
	4	20	.00	.00	1.33	8.98	21.82	13.04	.11	1.48	.00	.00	.00	.00	.00	.00
	3	15	.00	.10	5.96	19.01	20.54	7.16	.02	.46	.00	.00	.00	.00	.00	.00
	2	10	.00	1.59	18.87	28.51	13.69	2.78	.00	.11	.00	.00	.00	.00	.00	.00
	1	5	.00	16.52	37.74	27.01	5.76	.68	.00	.02	.00	.00	.00	.00	.00	.00
	0	0	100.00	81.79	35.85	12.16	1.15	.08	.00	.00	.00	.00	.00	.00	.00	.00
	Total		100.00	100.00	100.00	100.00	100.00	100.00	100.00	100.00	100.00	100.00	100.00	100.00	100.00	100.00

(continued)

Table A-2a (continued)

No. of items in test (n)	No. right (R)	% right	Percentage of cases											
			$P = .00$	$P = .01$	$P = .05$	$P = .10$	$P = .20$	$P = .30$	$P = .50$	$P = .70$	$P = .80$	$P = .90$	$P = .95$	$P = .99$	$P = 1.00$
40	40	100	.00	.00	.00	.00	.00	.00	.00	.00	.01	1.48	12.85	66.91	100.00
	39	97.5	.00	.00	.00	.00	.00	.00	.00	.00	.13	6.57	27.06	27.03	.00
	38	95	.00	.00	.00	.00	.00	.00	.00	.01	.65	14.23	27.76	5.32	.00
	37	92.5	.00	.00	.00	.00	.00	.00	.00	.05	2.05	20.03	18.51	.68	.00
	36	90	.00	.00	.00	.00	.00	.00	.00	.20	4.75	20.59	9.01	.06	.00
	35	87.5	.00	.00	.00	.00	.00	.00	.00	.61	8.54	16.47	3.42	.00	.00
	34	85	.00	.00	.00	.00	.00	.00	.00	1.51	12.46	10.68	1.05	.00	.00
	33	82.5	.00	.00	.00	.00	.00	.00	.00	3.15	15.13	5.76	.27	.00	.00
	32	80	.00	.00	.00	.00	.00	.00	.01	5.57	15.59	2.64	.06	.00	.00
	31	77.5	.00	.00	.00	.00	.00	.00	.02	8.49	13.86	1.04	.01	.00	.00
	30	75	.00	.00	.00	.00	.00	.00	.08	11.28	10.75	.36	.00	.00	.00
	29	72.5	.00	.00	.00	.00	.00	.00	.21	13.19	7.33	.11	.00	.00	.00
	28	70	.00	.00	.00	.00	.00	.00	.51	13.65	4.43	.03	.00	.00	.00
	27	67.5	.00	.00	.00	.00	.00	.00	1.09	12.61	2.38	.01	.00	.00	.00
	26	65	.00	.00	.00	.00	.00	.00	2.11	10.42	1.15	.00	.00	.00	.00
	25	62.5	.00	.00	.00	.00	.00	.00	3.66	7.74	.50	.00	.00	.00	.00
	24	60	.00	.00	.00	.00	.00	.01	5.72	5.18	.19	.00	.00	.00	.00
	23	57.5	.00	.00	.00	.00	.00	.02	8.07	3.14	.07	.00	.00	.00	.00

22	55	.00	.00	.00	.00	.00	.00	10.31	1.72	.02	.00	.00	.00
21	52.5	.00	.00	.00	.00	.00	.00	11.94	.85	.01	.00	.00	.00
20	50	.00	.00	.00	.00	.00	.00	12.54	.38	.00	.00	.00	.00
19	47.5	.00	.00	.00	.00	.01	.85	11.94	.16	.00	.00	.00	.00
18	45	.00	.00	.00	.00	.02	1.72	10.31	.06	.00	.00	.00	.00
17	42.5	.00	.00	.00	.00	.07	3.14	8.07	.02	.00	.00	.00	.00
16	40	.00	.00	.00	.00	.19	5.18	5.72	.01	.00	.00	.00	.00
15	37.5	.00	.00	.00	.00	.50	7.74	3.66	.00	.00	.00	.00	.00
14	35	.00	.00	.00	.00	1.15	10.42	2.11	.00	.00	.00	.00	.00
13	32.5	.00	.00	.00	.01	2.38	12.61	1.09	.00	.00	.00	.00	.00
12	30	.00	.00	.00	.03	4.43	13.65	.51	.00	.00	.00	.00	.00
11	27.5	.00	.00	.00	.11	7.33	13.19	.21	.00	.00	.00	.00	.00
10	25	.00	.00	.00	.36	10.75	11.28	.08	.00	.00	.00	.00	.00
9	22.5	.00	.00	.01	1.04	13.86	8.49	.02	.00	.00	.00	.00	.00
8	20	.00	.00	.06	2.64	15.59	5.57	.01	.00	.00	.00	.00	.00
7	17.5	.00	.00	.27	5.76	15.13	3.15	.00	.00	.00	.00	.00	.00
6	15	.00	.00	1.05	10.68	12.46	1.51	.00	.00	.00	.00	.00	.00
5	12.5	.00	.00	3.42	16.47	8.54	.61	.00	.00	.00	.00	.00	.00
4	10	.00	.00	9.01	20.59	4.75	.20	.00	.00	.00	.00	.00	.00
3	7.5	.00	.06	18.51	20.03	2.05	.05	.00	.00	.00	.00	.00	.00
2	5	.00	.68	27.76	14.23	.65	.01	.00	.00	.00	.00	.00	.00
1	2.5	.00	5.32	27.06	6.57	.13	.00	.00	.00	.00	.00	.00	.00
0	0	100.00	66.91	12.85	1.48	.01	.00	.00	.00	.00	.00	.00	.00
Total		100.00	100.00	100.00	100.00	100.00	100.00	100.00	100.00	100.00	100.00	100.00	100.00

Table A-2b. Theoretical Distribution of Scores on Criterion-referenced Multiple-choice Test Consisting of *Five-choice Items* for Individuals at Specified Levels of Competence.

No. of items in test (n)	No. right (R)	% right	P = .00	P = .01	P = .05	P = .10	P = .20	P = .30	P = .50	P = .70	P = .80	P = .90	P = .95	P = .99	P = 1.00
5	5	100	.00	.04	.08	.17	.60	1.65	7.78	25.36	41.82	65.91	81.53	96.07	100.00
	4	80	.00	.74	1.26	2.21	5.37	10.49	25.92	40.03	39.83	28.66	16.99	3.87	.00
	3	60	.00	5.64	7.98	11.38	19.11	26.71	34.56	25.29	15.17	4.98	1.42	.06	.00
	2	40	.00	21.49	25.29	29.26	33.98	34.00	23.04	7.98	2.89	.43	.06	.00	.00
	1	20	.00	40.93	40.03	37.63	30.20	21.64	7.68	1.26	.28	.02	.00	.00	.00
	0	0	100.00	31.16	25.36	19.35	10.74	5.51	1.02	.08	.01	.00	.00	.00	.00
	Total		100.00	100.00	100.00	100.00	100.00	100.00	100.00	100.00	100.00	100.00	100.00	100.00	100.00
10	10	100	.00	.00	.00	.00	.00	.03	.60	6.43	17.49	43.45	66.49	92.28	100.00
	9	90	.00	.00	.00	.01	.06	.35	4.03	20.30	33.31	37.77	27.70	7.44	.00
	8	80	.00	.01	.03	.09	.52	1.98	12.09	28.85	28.56	14.78	5.19	.27	.00
	7	70	.00	.10	.24	.60	2.47	6.73	21.50	24.29	14.50	3.43	.58	.01	.00
	6	60	.00	.67	1.34	2.72	7.67	14.99	25.08	13.43	4.83	.52	.04	.00	.00
	5	50	.00	3.06	5.09	8.39	16.36	22.89	20.07	5.09	1.11	.05	.00	.00	.00
	4	40	.00	9.70	13.43	17.98	24.24	24.27	11.15	1.34	.18	.00	.00	.00	.00
	3	30	.00	21.11	24.29	26.43	24.62	17.65	4.25	.24	.02	.00	.00	.00	.00
	2	20	.00	30.14	28.85	25.48	16.42	8.43	1.06	.03	.00	.00	.00	.00	.00
	1	10	.00	25.50	20.30	14.56	6.49	2.38	.16	.00	.00	.00	.00	.00	.00
	0	0	100.00	9.71	6.43	3.74	1.15	.30	.01	.00	.00	.00	.00	.00	.00
	Total		100.00	100.00	100.00	100.00	100.00	100.00	100.00	100.00	100.00	100.00	100.00	100.00	100.00

Percentage of cases

20	20	100	.00	.00	.00	.00	.00	.00	.00	.00	.00	18.87	44.20	85.16	100.00
	19	95	.00	.00	.00	.00	.00	.00	.00	.00	3.06	32.82	36.83	13.74	.00
	18	90	.00	.00	.00	.00	.00	.00	.00	.41	11.65	27.11	14.58	1.05	.00
	17	85	.00	.00	.00	.00	.00	.00	.05	2.61	21.09	14.14	3.64	.05	.00
	16	80	.00	.00	.00	.00	.00	.02	.31	7.83	24.09	5.23	.65	.00	.00
	15	75	.00	.00	.00	.00	.01	.09	1.23	14.84	19.51	1.45	.09	.00	.00
	14	70	.00	.00	.00	.01	.04	.38	3.50	19.91	11.89	.32	.01	.00	.00
	13	65	.00	.00	.01	.05	.16	1.22	7.46	20.11	5.66	.05	.00	.00	.00
	12	60	.00	.01	.05	.21	.58	3.10	12.44	15.89	2.16	.01	.00	.00	.00
	11	55	.00	.06	.22	.72	1.68	6.42	16.59	10.05	.67	.00	.00	.00	.00
	10	50	.00	.27	.75	2.05	3.98	10.89	17.98	5.15	.17	.00	.00	.00	.00
	9	45	.00	.94	2.17	4.79	7.79	15.24	17.64	2.17	.04	.00	.00	.00	.00
	8	40	.00	2.69	5.15	9.24	12.59	17.64	15.97	.75	.01	.00	.00	.00	.00
	7	35	.00	6.30	10.03	14.62	16.78	16.83	11.71	.22	.00	.00	.00	.00	.00
	6	30	.00	11.99	15.89	18.79	18.35	13.18	7.10	.05	.00	.00	.00	.00	.00
	5	25	.00	18.27	20.13	19.33	16.32	8.39	3.55	.01	.00	.00	.00	.00	.00
	4	20	.00	21.74	19.91	15.53	11.61	4.27	1.46	.00	.00	.00	.00	.00	.00
	3	15	.00	19.48	14.84	9.40	6.45	1.70	.49	.00	.00	.00	.00	.00	.00
	2	10	.00	12.36	7.83	4.03	2.70	.51	.13	.00	.00	.00	.00	.00	.00
	1	5	.00	4.95	2.61	1.09	.80	.11	.03	.00	.00	.00	.00	.00	.00
	0	0	100.00	.94	.41	.14	.15	.01	.00	.00	.00	.00	.00	.00	.00
	Total		100.00	100.00	100.00	100.00	100.00	100.00	100.00	100.00	100.00	100.00	100.00	100.00	100.00

(continued)

Table A-2b (continued)

No. of items in test (n)	No. right (R)	% right	Percentage of cases											
			P = .00	P = .01	P = .05	P = .10	P = .20	P = .30	P = .50	P = .70	P = .80	P = .90	P = .95	P = .99	P = 1.00
40	40	100	.00	.00	.00	.00	.00	.00	.00	.00	.09	3.56	19.54	72.52	100.00
	39	97.5	.00	.00	.00	.00	.00	.00	.00	.02	.71	12.38	32.57	23.39	.00
	38	95	.00	.00	.00	.00	.00	.00	.00	.13	2.65	21.00	26.46	3.68	.00
	37	92.5	.00	.00	.00	.00	.00	.00	.00	.53	6.39	23.13	13.96	.38	.00
	36	90	.00	.00	.00	.00	.00	.00	.00	1.55	11.26	18.60	5.38	.03	.00
	35	87.5	.00	.00	.00	.00	.00	.00	.01	3.53	15.45	11.65	1.61	.00	.00
	34	85	.00	.00	.00	.00	.00	.00	.05	6.50	17.15	5.91	.39	.00	.00
	33	82.5	.00	.00	.00	.00	.00	.00	.15	9.97	15.87	2.50	.08	.00	.00
	32	80	.00	.00	.00	.00	.00	.00	.40	12.99	12.47	.90	.01	.00	.00
	31	77.5	.00	.00	.00	.00	.00	.00	.95	14.60	8.44	.28	.00	.00	.00
	30	75	.00	.00	.00	.00	.00	.01	1.96	14.28	4.99	.07	.00	.00	.00
	29	72.5	.00	.00	.00	.00	.00	.02	3.57	12.30	2.59	.02	.00	.00	.00
	28	70	.00	.00	.00	.00	.00	.06	5.76	9.39	1.19	.00	.00	.00	.00
	27	67.5	.00	.00	.00	.00	.00	.15	8.27	6.38	.49	.00	.00	.00	.00
	26	65	.00	.00	.00	.00	.01	.37	10.63	3.89	.18	.00	.00	.00	.00
	25	62.5	.00	.00	.00	.00	.04	.82	12.27	2.13	.06	.00	.00	.00	.00

24	60	.00	.00	.00	.00	.00	.00	1.05	.02	.00	.00	.00	.00
23	57.5	.00	.00	.00	.00	.00	.00	12.78	1.63	.47	.00	.00	.00
22	55	.00	.00	.00	.01	.11	.00	12.04	2.93	.19	.00	.00	.00
21	52.5	.00	.00	.00	.02	.28	.01	10.26	4.76	.07	.00	.00	.00
20	50	.00	.00	.01	.06	.64	.02	7.92	7.02	.02	.00	.00	.00
19	47.5	.00	.01	.02	.17	1.31	.06	5.54	9.38	.01	.00	.00	.00
18	45	.00	.04	.07	.42	2.45	.17	3.52	11.37	.00	.00	.00	.00
17	42.5	.00	.11	.19	.92	4.15	.42	2.03	12.50	.00	.00	.00	.00
16	40	.00	.29	.47	1.86	6.37	.92	1.06	12.45	.00	.00	.00	.00
15	37.5	.00	.70	1.05	3.38	8.86	1.86	.50	11.22	.00	.00	.00	.00
14	35	.00	1.53	2.13	5.56	11.16	3.38	.21	9.14	.00	.00	.00	.00
13	32.5	.00	3.03	3.89	8.25	12.69	5.56	.08	6.71	.00	.00	.00	.00
12	30	.00	5.35	6.38	11.00	13.02	8.25	.03	4.43	.00	.00	.00	.00
11	27.5	.00	8.43	9.39	13.13	12.00	11.00	.01	2.62	.00	.00	.00	.00
10	25	.00	11.77	12.30	13.98	9.90	13.13	.00	1.38	.00	.00	.00	.00
9	22.5	.00	14.44	14.28	13.18	7.29	13.98	.00	.64	.00	.00	.00	.00
8	20	.00	15.47	14.60	10.93	4.75	13.18	.00	.26	.00	.00	.00	.00
7	17.5	.00	14.28	12.99	7.90	2.72	10.93	.00	.09	.00	.00	.00	.00
6	15	.00	11.20	9.97	4.93	1.36	7.90	.00	.03	.00	.00	.00	.00
5	12.5	.00	7.31	6.50	2.61	.59	4.93	.00	.01	.00	.00	.00	.00
4	10	.00	3.87	3.53	1.15	.21	2.61	.00	.00	.00	.00	.00	.00
3	7.5	.00	1.59	1.55	.41	.07	1.15	.00	.00	.00	.00	.00	.00
2	5	.00	.48	.53	.11	.02	.41	.00	.00	.00	.00	.00	.00
1	2.5	.00	.09	.13	.02	.00	.11	.00	.00	.00	.00	.00	.00
0	0	100.00	.01	.02	.00	.00	.02	.00	.00	.00	.00	.00	.00
Total		100.00	100.00	100.00	100.00	100.00	100.00	100.00	100.00	100.00	100.00	100.00	100.00

Table A-2c. Theoretical Distribution of Scores on Criterion-referenced Multiple-choice Test Consisting of *Four-choice Items* for Individuals at Specified Levels of Competence.

| No. of items in test (n) | No. right (R) | % right | Percentage of cases ||||||||||||
			$P = .00$	$P = .01$	$P = .05$	$P = .10$	$P = .20$	$P = .30$	$P = .50$	$P = .70$	$P = .80$	$P = .90$	$P = .95$	$P = .99$	$P = 1.00$
5	5	100	.00	.11	.20	.36	1.02	2.42	9.54	27.96	44.36	67.73	82.61	96.31	100.00
	4	80	.00	1.63	2.43	3.77	7.68	13.36	28.61	40.58	39.15	27.45	16.09	3.64	.00
	3	60	.00	9.41	12.06	15.64	23.04	29.54	34.33	23.57	13.82	4.45	1.25	.05	.00
	2	40	.00	27.14	29.90	32.48	34.56	32.65	20.60	6.84	2.44	.36	.05	.00	.00
	1	20	.00	39.13	37.05	33.74	25.92	18.04	6.18	.99	.22	.01	.00	.00	.00
	0	0	100.00	22.58	18.36	14.01	7.78	3.99	.74	.06	.01	.00	.00	.00	.00
	Total		100.00	100.00	100.00	100.00	100.00	100.00	100.00	100.00	100.00	100.00	100.00	100.00	100.00
10	10	100	.00	.00	.00	.00	.01	.06	.91	7.82	19.69	45.86	68.24	92.75	100.00
	9	90	.00	.00	.01	.03	.16	.65	5.46	22.69	34.75	37.18	26.59	7.01	.00
	8	80	.00	.05	.11	.26	1.06	3.21	14.73	29.66	27.59	13.57	4.66	.24	.00
	7	70	.00	.37	.70	1.41	4.25	9.47	23.57	22.95	12.98	2.93	.48	.00	.00
	6	60	.00	1.86	3.06	5.14	11.15	18.32	24.75	11.66	4.01	.42	.03	.00	.00
	5	50	.00	6.44	9.09	12.80	20.07	24.31	17.82	4.06	.85	.04	.00	.00	.00
	4	40	.00	15.47	18.77	22.16	25.08	22.38	8.91	.98	.12	.00	.00	.00	.00
	3	30	.00	25.49	26.58	26.31	21.50	14.14	3.06	.16	.01	.00	.00	.00	.00
	2	20	.00	27.57	24.70	20.48	12.09	5.86	.69	.02	.00	.00	.00	.00	.00
	1	10	.00	17.66	13.61	9.45	4.03	1.44	.09	.00	.00	.00	.00	.00	.00
	0	0	100.00	5.09	3.37	1.96	.60	.16	.01	.00	.00	.00	.00	.00	.00
	Total		100.00	100.00	100.00	100.00	100.00	100.00	100.00	100.00	100.00	100.00	100.00	100.00	100.00

20

20	.00	.00	.00	.00	.00	.00	.01	.61	3.88	21.03	46.56	86.03	100.00
19	.00	.00	.00	.00	.00	.00	.10	3.55	13.68	34.11	36.28	13.00	.00
18	.00	.00	.00	.00	.00	.00	.57	9.78	22.93	26.27	13.43	.93	.00
17	.00	.00	.00	.00	.00	.01	2.04	17.04	24.29	12.78	3.14	.04	.00
16	.00	.00	.00	.00	.03	.05	5.19	21.04	18.21	4.40	.52	.00	.00
15	.00	.00	.00	.01	.13	.25	9.97	19.55	10.28	1.14	.06	.00	.00
14	.00	.00	.01	.05	.49	.87	14.96	14.18	4.54	.23	.01	.00	.00
13	.00	.02	.07	.22	1.46	2.42	17.95	8.23	1.60	.04	.00	.00	.00
12	.00	.10	.27	.75	3.55	5.34	17.50	3.88	.46	.00	.00	.00	.00
11	.00	.38	.88	2.09	7.10	9.59	14.00	1.50	.11	.00	.00	.00	.00
10	.00	1.21	2.40	4.77	11.71	14.13	9.24	.48	.02	.00	.00	.00	.00
9	.00	3.16	5.41	9.01	15.97	17.18	5.04	.13	.00	.00	.00	.00	.00
8	.00	6.84	10.06	14.03	17.98	17.28	2.27	.03	.00	.00	.00	.00	.00
7	.00	12.13	15.35	17.93	16.59	14.31	.84	.00	.00	.00	.00	.00	.00
6	.00	17.49	19.03	18.61	12.44	9.74	.25	.00	.00	.00	.00	.00	.00
5	.00	20.17	18.86	15.47	7.46	5.38	.06	.01	.00	.00	.00	.00	.00
4	.00	18.18	14.60	10.04	3.50	2.38	.01	.00	.00	.00	.00	.00	.00
3	.00	12.33	8.51	4.91	1.23	.82	.00	.00	.00	.00	.00	.00	.00
2	.00	5.93	3.52	1.70	.31	.21	.00	.00	.00	.00	.00	.00	.00
1	.00	1.80	.92	.37	.05	.04	.00	.00	.00	.00	.00	.00	.00
0	100.00	.26	.11	.04	.00	.00	.00	.00	.00	.00	.00	.00	.00
Total	100.00	100.00	100.00	100.00	100.00	100.00	100.00	100.00	100.00	100.00	100.00	100.00	100.00

(continued)

Table A-2c (continued)

No. of items in test (n)	No. right (R)	% right	Percentage of cases											
			$P = .00$	$P = .01$	$P = .05$	$P = .10$	$P = .20$	$P = .30$	$P = .50$	$P = .70$	$P = .80$	$P = .90$	$P = .95$	$P = .99$	$P = 1.00$
40	40	100	.00	.00	.00	.00	.00	.00	.00	.00	.15	4.42	21.68	73.99	100.00
	39	97.5	.00	.00	.00	.00	.00	.00	.00	.04	1.06	14.34	33.77	22.37	.00
	38	95	.00	.00	.00	.00	.00	.00	.00	.25	3.65	22.68	25.67	3.30	.00
	37	92.5	.00	.00	.00	.00	.00	.00	.00	.90	8.16	23.29	12.67	.32	.00
	36	90	.00	.00	.00	.00	.00	.00	.01	2.42	13.32	17.47	4.57	.02	.00
	35	87.5	.00	.00	.00	.00	.00	.00	.04	5.07	16.91	10.20	1.28	.00	.00
	34	85	.00	.00	.00	.00	.00	.00	.12	8.58	17.41	4.82	.29	.00	.00
	33	82.5	.00	.00	.00	.00	.00	.00	.36	12.10	14.92	1.90	.06	.00	.00
	32	80	.00	.00	.00	.00	.00	.00	.88	14.49	10.87	.64	.01	.00	.00
	31	77.5	.00	.00	.00	.00	.00	.01	1.89	14.96	6.82	.18	.00	.00	.00
	30	75	.00	.00	.00	.00	.00	.03	3.51	13.46	3.73	.05	.00	.00	.00
	29	72.5	.00	.00	.00	.00	.00	.08	5.74	10.66	1.80	.01	.00	.00	.00
	28	70	.00	.00	.00	.00	.01	.22	8.32	7.48	.77	.00	.00	.00	.00
	27	67.5	.00	.00	.00	.00	.03	.52	10.75	4.68	.29	.00	.00	.00	.00
	26	65	.00	.00	.00	.00	.08	1.10| 12.44| 2.62	.10	.00	.00	.00	.00
	25	62.5	.00	.00	.00	.01	.21	2.11| 12.94| 1.32	.03	.00	.00	.00	.00
	24	60	.00	.00	.00	.02	.50	3.64| 12.13| .60	.01	.00	.00	.00	.00

23	57.5	.00	.00	.01	.07	1.06	5.69	10.28	.24	.00	.00	.00	.00
22	55	.00	.01	.03	.18	2.03	8.03	7.88	.09	.00	.00	.00	.00
21	52.5	.00	.02	.09	.42	3.52	10.28	5.47	.03	.00	.00	.00	.00
20	50	.00	.06	.23	.92	5.54	11.92	3.45	.01	.00	.00	.00	.00
19	47.5	.00	.16	.55	1.82	7.92	12.55	1.97	.00	.00	.00	.00	.00
18	45	.00	.40	1.18	3.26	10.26	11.98	1.02	.00	.00	.00	.00	.00
17	42.5	.00	.91	2.29	5.30	12.04	10.36	.48	.00	.00	.00	.00	.00
16	40	.00	1.85	4.01	7.79	12.78	8.11	.20	.00	.00	.00	.00	.00
15	37.5	.00	3.42	6.36	10.36	12.27	5.74	.08	.00	.00	.00	.00	.00
14	35	.00	5.68	9.10	12.41	10.63	3.66	.03	.00	.00	.00	.00	.00
13	32.5	.00	8.50	11.69	13.38	8.27	2.10	.01	.00	.00	.00	.00	.00
12	30	.00	11.38	13.45	12.89	5.76	1.08	.00	.00	.00	.00	.00	.00
11	27.5	.00	13.57	13.80	11.08	3.57	.49	.00	.00	.00	.00	.00	.00
10	25	.00	14.34	12.54	8.44	1.96	.20	.00	.00	.00	.00	.00	.00
9	22.5	.00	13.35	10.02	5.65	.95	.07	.00	.00	.00	.00	.00	.00
8	20	.00	10.83	6.99	3.30	.40	.02	.00	.00	.00	.00	.00	.00
7	17.5	.00	7.57	4.20	1.66	.15	.01	.00	.00	.00	.00	.00	.00
6	15	.00	4.49	2.14	.71	.05	.00	.00	.00	.00	.00	.00	.00
5	12.5	.00	2.22	.91	.25	.01	.00	.00	.00	.00	.00	.00	.00
4	10	.00	.89	.31	.07	.00	.00	.00	.00	.00	.00	.00	.00
3	7.5	.00	.28	.08	.02	.00	.00	.00	.00	.00	.00	.00	.00
2	5	.00	.06	.02	.00	.00	.00	.00	.00	.00	.00	.00	.00
1	2.5	.00	.01	.00	.00	.00	.00	.00	.00	.00	.00	.00	.00
0	0	100.00	.00	.00	.00	.00	.00	.00	.00	.00	.00	.00	.00
Total		100.00	100.00	100.00	100.00	100.00	100.00	100.00	100.00	100.00	100.00	100.00	100.00

Table A-2d. Theoretical Distribution of Scores on Criterion-referenced Multiple-choice Test Consisting of Three-choice Items for Individuals at Specified Levels of Competence.

No. of items in test (n)	No. right (R)	% right	Percentage of cases												
			$p=.00$	$p=.01$	$p=.05$	$p=.10$	$p=.20$	$p=.30$	$p=.50$	$p=.70$	$p=.80$	$p=.90$	$p=.95$	$p=.99$	$p=1.00$
5	5	100	.00	.45	.66	1.02	2.21	4.32	13.17	32.77	48.90	70.83	84.42	96.71	100.00
	4	80	.00	4.41	5.72	7.68	12.65	18.88	32.92	40.96	37.61	25.29	14.55	3.25	.00
	3	60	.00	17.12	19.77	23.04	28.91	33.03	32.92	20.48	11.57	3.61	1.00	.04	.00
	2	40	.00	33.24	34.16	34.56	33.03	28.91	16.46	5.12	1.78	.26	.03	.00	.00
	1	20	.00	32.26	29.50	25.92	18.88	12.65	4.12	.64	.14	.01	.00	.00	.00
	0	0	100.00	12.52	10.19	7.78	4.32	2.21	.41	.03	.00	.00	.00	.00	.00
	Total		100.00	100.00	100.00	100.00	100.00	100.00	100.00	100.00	100.00	100.00	100.00	100.00	100.00
10	10	100	.00	.00	.00	.01	.05	.19	1.73	10.74	23.91	50.17	71.25	93.53	100.00
	9	90	.00	.04	.08	.16	.56	1.63	8.67	26.84	36.77	35.83	24.57	6.28	.00
	8	80	.00	.35	.59	1.06	2.88	6.42	19.51	30.20	25.46	11.52	3.81	.19	.00
	7	70	.00	1.81	2.72	4.25	8.77	14.97	26.02	20.13	10.45	2.19	.35	.00	.00
	6	60	.00	6.16	8.21	11.15	17.55	22.92	22.76	8.81	2.81	.27	.02	.00	.00
	5	50	.00	14.34	17.02	20.07	24.06	24.06	13.66	2.64	.52	.02	.00	.00	.00
	4	40	.00	23.20	24.49	25.08	22.92	17.55	5.69	.55	.07	.00	.00	.00	.00
	3	30	.00	25.72	24.18	21.50	14.97	8.77	1.63	.08	.01	.00	.00	.00	.00
	2	20	.00	18.73	15.66	12.09	6.42	2.88	.30	.01	.00	.00	.00	.00	.00
	1	10	.00	8.08	6.01	4.03	1.63	.56	.03	.00	.00	.00	.00	.00	.00
	0	0	100.00	1.57	1.04	.60	.19	.05	.00	.00	.00	.00	.00	.00	.00
	Total		100.00	100.00	100.00	100.00	100.00	100.00	100.00	100.00	100.00	100.00	100.00	100.00	100.00

20																		
	20	100	.00	.00	.00	.00	.00	.00	.00	.00	.00	.00	.03	1.15	5.72	25.16	50.76	87.48	100.00
	19	95	.00	.00	.00	.00	.00	.00	.00	.00	.00	.01	.30	5.76	17.59	35.95	35.01	11.74	.00
	18	90	.00	.00	.00	.00	.00	.00	.00	.00	.01	.05	1.43	13.69	25.69	24.39	11.47	.75	.00
	17	85	.00	.00	.00	.00	.00	.00	.00	.01	.04	.26	4.29	20.54	23.72	10.45	2.37	.03	.00
	16	80	.00	.00	.00	.00	.00	.00	.01	.03	.20	.98	9.11	21.82	15.51	3.17	.35	.00	.00
	15	75	.00	.00	.00	.00	.00	.02	.05	.13	.73	2.76	14.57	17.46	7.64	.73	.04	.00	.00
	14	70	.00	.00	.00	.00	.02	.05	.20	.49	2.07	6.03	18.21	10.91	2.94	.13	.00	.00	.00
	13	65	.00	.00	.00	.02	.09	.20	.69	1.46	4.74	10.55	18.21	5.45	.90	.02	.00	.00	.00
	12	60	.00	.00	.02	.09	.34	.69	1.93	3.55	8.80	15.01	14.80	2.22	.23	.00	.00	.00	.00
	11	55	.00	.00	.09	.34	1.08	1.93	4.43	7.10	13.41	17.50	9.87	.74	.05	.00	.00	.00	.00
	10	50	.00	.00	.34	1.08	2.80	4.43	8.43	11.71	16.85	17.50	5.43	.20	.01	.00	.00	.00	.00
	9	45	.00	.00	1.08	2.80	5.98	8.43	13.23	15.97	17.50	13.41	2.47	.05	.00	.00	.00	.00	.00
	8	40	.00	.02	2.80	5.98	10.56	13.23	17.14	17.98	16.85	8.80	.92	.01	.00	.00	.00	.00	.00
	7	35	.00	.09	5.98	10.56	15.37	17.14	18.22	17.98	13.41	4.74	.28	.00	.00	.00	.00	.00	.00
	6	30	.00	.34	10.56	15.37	17.98	18.37	16.59	12.44	8.80	2.07	.07	.00	.00	.00	.00	.00	.00
	5	25	.00	1.08	15.37	18.22	17.98	15.37	12.44	7.46	4.74	.73	.01	.00	.00	.00	.00	.00	.00
	4	20	.00	2.80	17.82	17.14	12.44	10.87	7.46	3.50	2.07	.20	.00	.00	.00	.00	.00	.00	.00
	3	15	.00	8.39	15.73	12.44	5.87	3.50	2.76	1.23	.73	.04	.00	.00	.00	.00	.00	.00	.00
	2	10	.00	3.83	10.87	7.46	2.38	1.23	.98	.31	.20	.01	.00	.00	.00	.00	.00	.00	.00
	1	5	.00	1.24	3.83	2.38	.69	.31	.26	.05	.04	.00	.00	.00	.00	.00	.00	.00	.00
	0	0	.00	.25	.69	.31	.12	.05	.04	.01	.01	.00	.00	.00	.00	.00	.00	.00	.00
	Total		100.00	100.00	100.00	100.00	100.00	100.00	100.00	100.00	100.00	100.00	100.00	100.00	100.00	100.00	100.00	100.00	100.00

(continued)

Table A-2d (continued)

No. of items in test (n)	No. right (R)	% right	Percentage of cases										
			P = .00	P = .01	P = .05	P = .10	P = .20	P = .30	P = .50	P = .70	P = .80	P = .90	P = .95	P = .99	P = 1.00
40	40	100	.00	.00	.00	.00	.00	.00	.00	.01	.33	6.33	25.77	76.53	100.00
	39	97.5	.00	.00	.00	.00	.00	.00	.00	.13	2.01	18.09	35.53	20.54	.00
	38	95	.00	.00	.00	.00	.00	.00	.00	.65	6.03	25.19	23.90	2.69	.00
	37	92.5	.00	.00	.00	.00	.00	.00	.01	2.05	11.75	22.80	10.44	.23	.00
	36	90	.00	.00	.00	.00	.00	.00	.05	4.75	16.72	15.06	3.33	.01	.00
	35	87.5	.00	.00	.00	.00	.00	.00	.19	8.54	18.52	7.75	.83	.00	.00
	34	85	.00	.00	.00	.00	.00	.00	.54	12.46	16.62	3.23	.17	.00	.00
	33	82.5	.00	.00	.00	.00	.00	.01	1.32	15.13	12.42	1.12	.03	.00	.00
	32	80	.00	.00	.00	.00	.00	.03	2.72	15.59	7.88	.33	.00	.00	.00
	31	77.5	.00	.00	.00	.00	.01	.10	4.83	13.86	4.31	.08	.00	.00	.00
	30	75	.00	.00	.00	.00	.02	.27	7.49	10.75	2.06	.02	.00	.00	.00
	29	72.5	.00	.00	.00	.00	.06	.64	10.21	7.33	.86	.00	.00	.00	.00
	28	70	.00	.00	.00	.01	.16	1.35| 12.34| 4.43	.32	.00	.00	.00	.00
	27	67.5	.00	.00	.01	.03	.39	2.55| 13.29| 2.38	.11	.00	.00	.00	.00
	26	65	.00	.00	.02	.08	.87	4.30| 12.81| 1.15	.03	.00	.00	.00	.00
	25	62.5	.00	.02	.05	.21	1.72	6.52	11.10	.50	.01	.00	.00	.00	.00
	24	60	.00	.05	.15	.50	3.07| 8.92| 8.67	.19	.00	.00	.00	.00	.00
	23	57.5	.00	.13	.36	1.06	4.95	11.02	6.12	.07	.00	.00	.00	.00	.00

142

22	55	.00	.00								.00
21	52.5	.00	.00								.00
20	50	.00	.00								.00
19	47.5	.00	.00								.00
18	45	.00	.00								.00
17	42.5	.00	.00								.00
16	40	.00	.00								.00
15	37.5	.00	.00								.00
14	35	.00	.00								.00
13	32.5	.00	.00								.00
12	30	.00	.00								.00
11	27.5	.00	.32	.79	2.03	7.22	12.32	3.91	.02	.00	.00	.00
10	25	.00	.71	1.58	3.52	9.56	12.47	2.26	.01	.00	.00	.00
9	22.5	.00	1.44	2.87	5.54	11.47	11.47	1.19	.00	.00	.00	.00
8	20	.00	2.67	4.72	7.92	12.47	9.56	.57	.00	.00	.00	.00
7	17.5	.00	4.48	7.04	10.26	12.32	7.22	.24	.00	.00	.00	.00
6	15	.00	6.80	9.51	12.04	11.02	4.95	.10	.00	.00	.00	.00
5	12.5	.00	9.35	11.64	12.78	8.92	3.07	.03	.00	.00	.00	.00
4	10	.00	11.62	12.85	12.27	6.52	1.72	.01	.00	.00	.00	.00
3	7.5	.00	13.02	12.82	10.63	4.30	.87	.00	.00	.00	.00	.00
2	5	.00	13.10	11.48	8.27	2.55	.39	.00	.00	.00	.00	.00
1	2.5	.00	11.81	9.21	5.76	1.35	.16	.00	.00	.00	.00	.00
0	0	.00	9.48	6.58	3.57	.64	.06	.00	.00	.00	.00	.00
		.00	6.75	4.17	1.96	.27	.02	.00	.00	.00	.00	.00
		.00	4.23	2.32	.95	.10	.01	.00	.00	.00	.00	.00
		.00	2.31	1.13	.40	.03	.00	.00	.00	.00	.00	.00
		.00	1.09	.47	.15	.01	.00	.00	.00	.00	.00	.00
		.00	.43	.17	.05	.00	.00	.00	.00	.00	.00	.00
		.00	.14	.05	.01	.00	.00	.00	.00	.00	.00	.00
		.00	.04	.01	.00	.00	.00	.00	.00	.00	.00	.00
		.00	.01	.00	.00	.00	.00	.00	.00	.00	.00	.00
		.00	.00	.00	.00	.00	.00	.00	.00	.00	.00	.00
		100.00	.00	.00	.00	.00	.00	.00	.00	.00	.00	.00
Total		100.00	100.00	100.00	100.00	100.00	100.00	100.00	100.00	100.00	100.00	100.00

Table A-2e. Theoretical Distribution of Scores on Criterion-referenced Multiple-choice Test Consisting of *Two-choice Items* for Individuals at Specified Levels of Competence.

No. of items in test (n)	No. right (R)	% right	Percentage of cases										
			P = .00	P = .01	P = .05	P = .10	P = .20	P = .30	P = .50	P = .70	P = .80	P = .90	P = .95	P = .99	P = 1.00
5	5	100	.00	3.28	3.99	5.03	7.78	11.60	23.73	44.36	59.06	77.39	88.11	97.53	100.00
	4	80	.00	16.10	18.04	20.59	25.92	31.24	39.55	39.15	32.80	20.36	11.30	2.45	.00
	3	60	.00	31.56	32.65	33.68	34.56	33.64	26.37	13.82	7.29	2.14	.58	.02	.00
	2	40	.00	30.93	29.54	27.57	23.04	18.11	8.79	2.44	.81	.11	.01	.00	.00
	1	20	.00	15.16	13.36	11.28	7.68	4.88	1.46	.22	.04	.00	.00	.00	.00
	0	0	100.00	2.97	2.42	1.85	1.02	.53	.10	.01	.00	.00	.00	.00	.00
	Total		100.00	100.00	100.00	100.00	100.00	100.00	100.00	100.00	100.00	100.00	100.00	100.00	100.00
10	10	100	.00	.11	.16	.25	.60	1.35	5.63	19.69	34.87	59.87	77.62	95.11	100.00
	9	90	.00	1.06	1.44	2.07	4.03	7.25	18.77	34.75	38.74	31.51	19.91	4.78	.00
	8	80	.00	4.66	5.86	7.63	12.09	17.57	28.16	27.59	19.37	7.46	2.30	.11	.00
	7	70	.00	12.19	14.14	16.65	21.50	25.21	25.03	12.98	5.74	1.05	.16	.00	.00
	6	60	.00	20.91	22.38	23.84	25.08	23.77	14.60	4.01	1.12	.10	.01	.00	.00
	5	50	.00	24.60	24.31	23.40	20.07	15.36	5.84	.85	.15	.01	.00	.00	.00
	4	40	.00	20.09	18.32	15.96	11.15	6.89	1.62	.12	.01	.00	.00	.00	.00
	3	30	.00	11.25	9.47	7.46	4.25	2.12	.31	.01	.00	.00	.00	.00	.00
	2	20	.00	4.14	3.21	2.29	1.06	.43	.04	.00	.00	.00	.00	.00	.00
	1	10	.00	.90	.65	.42	.16	.05	.00	.00	.00	.00	.00	.00	.00
	0	0	100.00	.09	.06	.03	.01	.00	.00	.00	.00	.00	.00	.00	.00
	Total		100.00	100.00	100.00	100.00	100.00	100.00	100.00	100.00	100.00	100.00	100.00	100.00	100.00

20													
	20	100	.00	.00	.00	.00	.02	.32	3.88	12.16	35.85	60.26	90.47	100.00
	19	95	.00	.00	.00	.01	.05	2.11	13.68	27.01	37.74	30.91	9.09	.00
	18	90	.00	.02	.04	.08	.31	6.69	22.93	28.51	18.87	7.53	.43	.00
	17	85	.00	.12	.21	.40	1.23	13.39	24.29	19.01	5.96	1.16	.01	.00
	16	80	.00	.52	.82	1.39	3.50	18.97	18.21	8.98	1.33	.13	.00	.00
	15	75	.00	1.63	2.38	3.65	7.46	20.23	10.28	3.19	.22	.01	.00	.00
	14	70	.00	4.00	5.38	7.46	12.44	16.86	4.54	.89	.03	.00	.00	.00
	13	65	.00	7.84	9.74	12.21	16.59	11.24	1.60	.20	.00	.00	.00	.00
	12	60	.00	12.49	14.31	16.23	17.98	6.09	.46	.04	.00	.00	.00	.00
	11	55	.00	16.33	17.28	17.72	15.97	2.71	.11	.01	.00	.00	.00	.00
	10	50	.00	17.60	17.18	15.93	11.71	.99	.02	.00	.00	.00	.00	.00
	9	45	.00	15.69	14.13	11.85	7.10	.30	.00	.00	.00	.00	.00	.00
	8	40	.00	11.53	9.59	7.27	3.55	.08	.00	.00	.00	.00	.00	.00
	7	35	.00	6.96	5.34	3.66	1.46	.02	.00	.00	.00	.00	.00	.00
	6	30	.00	3.41	2.42	1.50	.45	.00	.00	.00	.00	.00	.00	.00
	5	25	.00	1.34	.87	.49	.12	.00	.00	.00	.00	.00	.00	.00
	4	20	.00	.41	.25	.13	.03	.00	.00	.00	.00	.00	.00	.00
	3	15	.00	.09	.05	.03	.00	.00	.00	.00	.00	.00	.00	.00
	2	10	.00	.02	.01	.00	.00	.00	.00	.00	.00	.00	.00	.00
	1	5	.00	.00	.00	.00	.00	.00	.00	.00	.00	.00	.00	.00
	0	0	100.00	.00	.00	.00	.00	.00	.00	.00	.00	.00	.00	.00
Total			100.00	100.00	100.00	100.00	100.00	100.00	100.00	100.00	100.00	100.00	100.00	100.00

(continued)

Table A-2e (continued)

No. of items in test (n)	No. right (R)	% right	Percentage of cases											
			$P=.00$	$P=.01$	$P=.05$	$P=.10$	$P=.20$	$P=.30$	$P=.50$	$P=.70$	$P=.80$	$P=.90$	$P=.95$	$P=.99$	$P=1.00$
40	40	100	.00	.00	.00	.00	.00	.00	.00	.15	1.48	12.85	36.33	81.84	100.00
	39	97.5	.00	.00	.00	.00	.00	.00	.01	1.06	6.57	27.06	37.26	16.45	.00
	38	95	.00	.00	.00	.00	.00	.00	.09	3.65	14.23	27.76	18.63	1.61	.00
	37	92.5	.00	.00	.00	.00	.00	.01	.37	8.16	20.03	18.51	6.05	.10	.00
	36	90	.00	.00	.00	.00	.00	.03	1.13	13.32	20.59	9.01	1.43	.00	.00
	35	87.5	.00	.00	.00	.00	.01	.10	2.72	16.91	16.47	3.42	.26	.00	.00
	34	85	.00	.00	.00	.00	.05	.31	5.30	17.41	10.68	1.05	.04	.00	.00
	33	82.5	.00	.00	.01	.01	.15	.80	8.57	14.92	5.76	.27	.00	.00	.00
	32	80	.00	.00	.02	.02	.40	1.79	11.79	10.87	2.64	.06	.00	.00	.00
	31	77.5	.00	.01	.07	.06	.95	3.42	13.98	6.82	1.04	.01	.00	.00	.00
	30	75	.00	.03	.20	.18	1.96	5.71	14.45	3.73	.36	.00	.00	.00	.00
	29	72.5	.00	.09	.49	.47	3.57	8.36	13.12	1.80	.11	.00	.00	.00	.00
	28	70	.00	.25	1.08	1.05	5.76	10.90	10.57	.77	.03	.00	.00	.00	.00
	27	67.5	.00	.60	2.10	2.07	8.27	12.65	7.59	.29	.01	.00	.00	.00	.00
	26	65	.00	1.26	3.66	3.65	10.63	13.14	4.88	.10	.00	.00	.00	.00	.00
	25	62.5	.00	2.38	5.74	5.75	12.27	12.26	2.82	.03	.00	.00	.00	.00	.00
	24	60	.00	4.04	8.11	8.16	12.78	10.31	1.47	.01	.00	.00	.00	.00	.00
			.00	6.18		10.43									

23	57.5	.00	8.55	10.36	12.05	12.04	7.84	.69	.00	.00	.00	.00
22	55	.00	10.71	11.98	12.60	10.26	5.39	.29	.00	.00	.00	.00
21	52.5	.00	12.16	12.55	11.94	7.92	3.36	.11	.00	.00	.00	.00
20	50	.00	12.50	11.92	10.25	5.54	1.90	.04	.00	.00	.00	.00
19	47.5	.00	12.68	10.28	7.99	3.52	.97	.01	.00	.00	.00	.00
18	45	.00	11.89	8.03	5.65	2.03	.45	.00	.00	.00	.00	.00
17	42.5	.00	9.89	5.69	3.62	1.06	.19	.00	.00	.00	.00	.00
16	40	.00	7.58	3.64	2.10	.50	.07	.00	.00	.00	.00	.00
15	37.5	.00	5.27	2.11	1.10	.21	.03	.00	.00	.00	.00	.00
14	35	.00	3.30	1.10	.52	.08	.01	.00	.00	.00	.00	.00
13	32.5	.00	1.87	.52	.22	.03	.00	.00	.00	.00	.00	.00
12	30	.00	.95	.22	.08	.01	.00	.00	.00	.00	.00	.00
11	27.5	.00	.43	.08	.03	.00	.00	.00	.00	.00	.00	.00
10	25	.00	.18	.03	.01	.00	.00	.00	.00	.00	.00	.00
9	22.5	.00	.06	.01	.00	.00	.00	.00	.00	.00	.00	.00
8	20	.00	.02	.00	.00	.00	.00	.00	.00	.00	.00	.00
7	17.5	.00	.01	.00	.00	.00	.00	.00	.00	.00	.00	.00
6	15	.00	.00	.00	.00	.00	.00	.00	.00	.00	.00	.00
5	12.5	.00	.00	.00	.00	.00	.00	.00	.00	.00	.00	.00
4	10	.00	.00	.00	.00	.00	.00	.00	.00	.00	.00	.00
3	7.5	.00	.00	.00	.00	.00	.00	.00	.00	.00	.00	.00
2	5	.00	.00	.00	.00	.00	.00	.00	.00	.00	.00	.00
1	2.5	.00	.00	.00	.00	.00	.00	.00	.00	.00	.00	.00
0	0	100.00	.00	.00	.00	.00	.00	.00	.00	.00	.00	.00
Total		100.00	100.00	100.00	100.00	100.00	100.00	100.00	100.00	100.00	100.00	100.00

Table A-3. Proportion of Cases at Various Levels of Competence Who Would Pass, and Proportion Who Would Fail, with Various Cutting Scores.

Cutting score (%)	Competence level (P)	For 10-item test											Based on Table A-2 data with P values as follows:
		Percentage passing and percentage failing											
		2-choice items		3-choice items		4-choice items		5-choice items		Constructed-answer items		
		Pass	Fail	Pass	Fail	Pass	Fail	Pass	Fail	Pass	Fail	
100	95–100	86.36	13.64	82.39	17.61	80.50	19.50	79.38	20.62	75.16	24.84	.95, .99
	85–95	59.87	40.13	50.17	49.83	45.86	54.14	43.45	56.55	34.87	65.13	.90
	75–85	34.87	65.13	23.91	76.09	19.69	80.31	17.49	82.51	10.74	89.26	.80
	65–75	19.69	80.31	10.74	89.26	7.82	92.18	6.43	93.57	2.82	97.18	.70
	55–65	12.66	87.34	6.24	93.76	4.36	95.64	3.52	96.48	1.46	98.54	.50, .70
	45–55	5.63	94.37	1.73	98.27	.91	99.09	.60	99.40	.10	99.90	.50
	35–45	3.49	96.51	.96	99.04	.48	99.52	.31	99.69	.05	99.95	.30, .50
	25–35	1.35	98.65	.19	99.81	.06	99.94	.03	99.97	.00	100.00	.30
	15–25	.60	99.40	.05	99.95	.01	99.99	.00	100.00	.00	100.00	.20
	5–15	.25	99.75	.01	99.99	.00	100.00	.00	100.00	.00	100.00	.10
	0–5	.14	99.86	.00	100.00	.00	100.00	.00	100.00	.00	100.00	.01, .05
90	95–100	98.71	1.29	97.82	2.18	97.30	2.70	96.95	3.05	95.48	4.52	.95, .99
	85–95	91.38	8.62	86.00	14.00	83.04	16.96	81.22	18.78	73.61	26.39	.90
	75–85	73.61	26.39	60.68	39.32	54.44	45.56	50.80	49.20	37.58	62.42	.80
	65–75	54.44	45.55	37.58	62.42	30.51	69.49	26.73	73.27	14.93	85.07	.70
	55–65	39.42	60.58	23.99	76.01	18.44	81.56	15.68	84.32	8.00	92.00	.50, .70
	45–55	24.40	75.60	10.40	89.60	6.37	93.73	4.63	95.37	1.08	98.92	.50
	35–45	16.50	83.50	6.11	93.89	3.54	96.46	2.50	97.50	.54	99.46	.30, .50
	25–35	8.60	91.40	1.82	98.18	.71	99.29	.38	99.62	.01	99.99	.30
	15–25	4.63	95.37	.61	99.39	.17	99.83	.06	99.94	.00	100.00	.20
	5–15	2.32	97.68	.17	99.83	.03	99.97	.01	99.99	.00	100.00	.10
	0–5	1.38	98.62	.06	99.94	.01	99.99	.00	100.00	.00	100.00	.01, .05

		.95, .99
		.90
		.80
		.70
		.50, .70
		.50
		.30, .50
		.30
		.20
		.10
		.01, .05

80											
	95-100	99.92	.08	99.82	.18	99.74	.26	99.68	.32	99.42	.58
	85-95	98.84	1.16	97.52	2.48	96.61	3.39	96.00	4.00	92.98	7.02
	75-85	92.98	7.02	86.14	13.86	82.03	17.97	79.36	20.64	67.78	32.22
	65-75	82.03	17.97	67.78	32.22	60.17	39.83	55.58	44.42	38.28	61.72
	55-65	67.30	32.70	48.85	51.15	40.64	59.36	36.15	63.85	21.88	78.12
	45-55	52.56	47.44	29.91	70.09	21.10	78.90	16.72	83.28	5.47	94.53
	35-45	39.36	60.64	19.07	80.93	12.51	87.49	9.54	90.46	2.81	97.19
	25-35	26.17	73.83	8.24	91.76	3.92	96.08	2.36	97.64	.15	99.85
	15-25	16.72	83.28	3.49	96.51	1.23	98.77	.58	99.42	.01	99.99
	5-15	9.95	90.05	1.23	98.77	.29	99.71	.10	99.90	.00	100.00
	0-5	6.64	93.36	.53	99.47	.08	99.92	.02	99.98	.00	100.00

70											
	95-100	100.00	.00	99.99	.01	99.98	.02	99.98	.02	99.95	.05
	85-95	99.89	.11	99.71	.29	99.54	.46	99.43	.57	98.72	1.28
	75-85	98.72	1.28	96.59	3.41	95.01	4.99	93.86	6.14	87.91	12.09
	65-75	95.01	4.99	87.91	12.09	83.12	16.88	79.87	20.13	64.96	35.04
	55-65	86.30	13.70	71.92	28.08	63.90	36.10	59.05	40.95	41.08	58.92
	45-55	77.59	22.41	55.93	44.07	44.67	55.33	38.22	61.78	17.19	82.81
	35-45	64.48	35.52	39.57	60.43	28.98	71.02	23.65	76.35	9.12	90.88
	25-35	51.38	48.62	23.21	76.79	13.39	86.61	9.09	90.91	1.05	98.95
	15-25	38.22	61.78	12.26	87.74	5.48	94.52	3.05	96.95	.09	99.91
	5-15	26.60	73.40	5.48	94.52	1.70	98.30	.70	99.30	.00	100.00
	0-5	19.81	80.19	2.80	97.20	.62	99.38	.19	99.81	.00	100.00

60											
	95-100	100.00	.00	100.00	.00	100.00	.00	100.00	.00	100.00	.00
	85-95	99.99	.01	99.98	.02	99.96	.04	99.95	.05	99.84	.16
	75-85	99.84	.16	99.40	.60	99.02	.98	98.63	1.37	96.92	3.28
	65-75	99.02	.98	96.72	3.28	94.78	5.22	93.30	6.70	84.97	15.03
	55-65	95.60	4.40	87.70	12.30	82.10	17.90	78.30	21.70	60.84	39.16
	45-55	92.19	7.81	78.69	21.31	69.42	30.58	63.30	36.70	36.70	63.30
	35-45	83.67	16.33	62.41	37.59	50.56	49.44	43.69	56.31	20.72	79.28
	25-35	75.15	24.85	46.13	53.87	31.71	68.29	24.08	75.92	4.73	95.27
	15-25	63.30	36.70	29.81	70.19	16.63	83.37	10.72	89.28	.64	99.36
	5-15	50.44	49.56	16.63	83.37	6.84	93.16	3.42	96.58	.01	99.99
	0-5	41.46	58.54	9.98	90.02	3.08	96.92	1.20	98.80	.00	100.00

Table A-4. Distributions Indicating Hypothetical Percentages of Population at Various Levels of Competence,[a] at Five Different Stages.[b]

Competence level (% mastery of domain)	Percentage of population				
	Stage 1 (preinstruction)	Stage 2	Stage 3	Stage 4	Stage 5
95–100	.00	.10	1.30	6.71	19.37
85– 95	.00	.98	7.16	21.81	38.74
75– 85	.00	4.39	17.56	30.20	27.98
65– 75	.00	11.72	25.36	23.91	10.85
55– 65	.05	20.51	23.90	12.12	2.60
45– 55	.41	24.60	15.36	4.13	.41
35– 45	2.60	20.51	6.82	.96	.05
25– 35	10.85	11.72	2.07	.15	.00
15– 25	27.98	4.39	.41	.01	.00
5– 15	38.74	.98	.05	.00	.00
0– 5	19.37	.10	.01	.00	.00
Total	100.00	100.00	100.00	100.00	100.00

[a]To develop these hypothetical distributions, the assumption that competence level has a continuous distribution has been imposed on an underlying binomial distribution for which $n = 9$, with each of the ten levels of the resulting point distribution corresponding to a break point between intervals of the hypothetical continuous distribution. It should be pointed out that there is no particular theoretical reason for using a binominal distribution for this purpose. It was selected because it was a convenient way of getting distributions with about the right sort of skew.

[b]The p values assumed for these binomial distributions for the five stages presented have been set at .10, .50, .667, .80, and .90 respectively.

2. *False failure.* This occurs when an examinee whose competency level is *at or above* the standard that has been set scores *below* the cutting point.

Table A-6 summarizes the data of Table A-5, by combining false passes with false failures, to yield overall misclassification rates at various stages with various cutting scores. Optimum cutting scores are determined weighting false passes and false failures equally; they are also determined for situations in which false passes are considered to be more serious than false failures, and consequently are weighted more heavily; and they are determined conversely for

Table A-5. Percentage Distribution of Classification Categories, at Various Stages with Various Kinds of Tests and Various Cutting Scores.

		% correct classifications												% misclassifications									
		Pass						Fail						False pass						False failure			
Kind of test	Cutting score (% right)	Stage						Stage						Stage						Stage				
		1	2	3	4	5		1	2	3	4	5		1	2	3	4	5		1	2	3	4	5
Constructed-answer items	100	.0	.4	3.6	13.7	31.0		100.0	98.0	88.9	67.6	38.6		.0	.9	2.7	3.9	3.3		.0	.7	4.8	14.8	27.1
	90	.0	.8	6.6	22.6	47.8		100.0	94.8	80.7	56.4	29.8		.0	4.1	10.9	15.1	12.1		.0	.3	1.8	5.9	10.3
	80	.0	1.0	8.0	26.9	55.4		99.8	87.8	67.4	40.9	18.6		.2	11.1	24.2	30.6	23.3		.0	.1	.4	1.6	2.7
	70	.0	1.1	8.4	28.1	57.6		99.3	76.0	51.7	26.5	9.7		.7	22.9	39.9	45.0	32.2		.0	.0	.0	.4	.5
	60	.0	1.1	8.4	28.5	58.0		98.1	59.4	35.6	15.5	4.5		1.9	39.5	56.0	56.0	37.4		.0	.0	.0	.0	.1
2-choice items	100	.0	.7	5.5	19.4	41.7		99.4	91.2	77.8	55.3	29.8		.6	7.7	13.8	16.2	12.1		.0	.4	2.9	9.1	16.4
	90	.0	.9	7.8	26.6	54.7		95.9	72.1	53.4	32.0	14.6		4.1	26.8	38.2	39.5	27.3		.0	.2	.6	1.9	3.4
	80	.0	1.1	8.3	38.3	57.7		85.9	46.8	29.6	14.7	5.4		14.1	52.1	62.0	56.8	36.5		.0	.0	.1	.2	.4
	70	.0	1.1	8.4	28.3	58.1		67.6	24.6	13.2	5.5	1.6		32.4	74.3	78.4	66.0	40.3		.0	.0	.0	.0	.0
	60	.0	1.1	8.4	28.5	58.1		44.2	10.3	4.6	1.7	.4		55.8	88.6	87.0	69.8	41.5		.0	.0	.0	.0	.0

NOTE: Desired standard of competence: $P = .85$
No. of test items: $n = 10$

Table A-6. Relative Amount of Misclassification at Various Stages with Various Cutting Scores.

Kind of test	Cutting score (% right)	Total % misclassification					Relative amount of misclassification with false passes and false failures weighted unequally[b]									
		False passes and false failures weighted equally					False passes weighted double					False failures weighted double				
		1	2	Stage 3	4	5	1	2	Stage 3	4	5	1	2	Stage 3	4	5
Constructed-answer items	100	.0[a]	1.6[a]	7.5[a]	18.7[a]	30.4	.0[a]	2.5[a]	10.2[a]	22.6[a]	33.7[a]	.0[a]	2.3[a]	12.3[a]	33.5	57.5
	90	.0	4.4	12.7	21.0	22.4[a]	.0	8.5	23.6	36.1	34.5	.0	4.7	14.5	26.9[a]	32.7
	80	.2	11.2	24.6	32.2	26.0	.4	22.3	48.8	62.8	49.3	.2	11.3	25.0	33.8	28.7[a]
	70	.7	22.9	39.9	45.4	32.7	1.4	45.8	79.8	90.4	64.9	.7	22.9	39.9	45.8	33.2
	60	1.9	39.5	56.0	56.0	37.5	3.8	79.0	112.0	112.0	74.9	1.9	39.5	56.0	56.0	37.6
2-choice items	100	.6[a]	8.1[a]	16.7[a]	25.3[a]	28.5[a]	1.2[a]	15.8[a]	30.5[a]	41.5[a]	40.6[a]	.6[a]	8.5[a]	19.6[a]	34.4[a]	44.9
	90	4.1	27.0	38.8	41.4	30.7	8.2	53.8	77.0	80.9	58.0	4.1	27.2	39.4	43.3	34.1[a]
	80	14.1	52.1	62.1	57.0	36.9	28.2	104.2	124.1	114.0	73.4	14.1	52.1	62.2	57.2	37.3
	70	32.4	74.3	78.4	66.0	40.3	64.8	148.6	156.8	132.0	80.6	32.4	74.3	78.4	66.0	40.3
	60	55.8	88.6	87.0	69.8	41.5	111.6	177.2	174.0	139.6	83.0	55.8	88.6	87.0	69.8	41.5

NOTE: Desired standard of competence: $P = .85$
No. of test items: $n = 10$

[a]This is at the optimum cutting score.
[b]Because of the weighting, these numbers should not be regarded as percentages.

Appendix A

situations where false failures are more serious and are therefore weighted more heavily.

It should be noted that no empirical data are used in the development of any of the tables, or in the determination of optimal cutting scores in various situations. The tables are based entirely on theoretical formulas. It should also be noted that the assumptions that are necessary in order to apply these formulas are minimal and reasonable.

RESULTS AND CONCLUSIONS

The theoretical distributions and the optimal cutting scores obtained as shown in the tables have interesting implications, not the least of which is the paradox referred to in the title of this appendix. The optimum cutting point does not generally coincide with the standard set for mastery of the domain. For instance, Tables A-5 and A-6 are based on the assumption that the standard for "mastery" has been set at 85%. But in the early stages, 100% is the optimum cutting score, while in stage 5 it goes down to 90% (or even to 80% if the situation is such that false failures are considered more serious than false passes). Thus the more competent the group as a whole, the *lower* the cutting score that may be set. It should be noted that these somewhat paradoxical results apply to an even greater extent when the test is of the constructed-answer type than when it is multiple-choice; thus chance success is not an important factor.

EDUCATIONAL IMPORTANCE

The finding that to minimize misclassification the cutting score should be set higher when the test is administered *before* instruction than when it is administered after instruction may have considerable practical significance in the application of criterion-referenced tests.

Furthermore, the finding may have significance considerably beyond the terms in which it has been stated. For instance, the authorities in degree-granting institutions that offer both internal degrees (earned by completing courses) and external degrees (earned primarily by examination, without specific course requirements) might want to consider this finding carefully, in setting passing grades on their criterion-referenced tests (and even, perhaps, on their norm-referenced tests!). And of course high schools and colleges that permit exemption from required courses on the basis of an examination should also take the finding into consideration. When requirements are met by examination only, as a substitute for course attendance plus examination, perhaps it is desirable to set the passing mark somewhat higher.

NOTE

[1] This is a slightly revised and somewhat expanded version of a paper that was presented by the author of this book at the Annual Meeting of the American Educational Research Association in San Francisco, 23 April 1976.

APPENDIX B.
The "accuracy analogues" of various standard statistics

This appendix contains the derivation of various "accuracy analogue" statistics, and summarizes the formulas. Table B-1 summarizes the notation used in this appendix to represent variables of various kinds.

Basically an accuracy analogue of a conventional statistic is a statistic that takes into account the absolute meaning of scores, not just their relative meaning. Therefore it should be particularly appropriate to criterion-referenced tests.

Table B-1. Summary of Notation Used in Appendix B to Represent Variables.

	Notation for variable		Notation for population mean	
Variable	Test A	Test B	Test A	Test B
Obtained score of individual i on test	a	b	$\bar{a}$	$\bar{b}$
True score of individual i on test	α	β	$\bar{\alpha}$	$\bar{\beta}$
Random error (error of measurement) of test score of individual i	ϵ	ω	$\bar{\epsilon}$	$\bar{\omega}$
Absolute score on underlying function measured by test	A	B	$\bar{A}$	$\bar{B}$

(continued)

Table B-1 (continued)

Variable	Notation for variable		Notation for population mean	
	Test A	Test B	Test A	Test B
Systematic error of test as an indicator of absolute score on underlying function	δ	Δ	$\bar{\delta}$	$\bar{\Delta}$
Total error of test score (= total deviation of test score from absolute score on underlying function)	d	D	$\bar{d}$	$\bar{D}$

Basic formulas

$$a = \alpha + \epsilon \tag{1a}$$
$$b = \beta + \omega \tag{1b}$$

$$\therefore \epsilon = a - \alpha \tag{2a}$$
$$\omega = b - \beta \tag{2b}$$

$$\alpha = A + \delta \tag{3a}$$
$$\beta = B + \Delta \tag{3b}$$

$$\therefore \delta = \alpha - A \tag{4a}$$
$$\Delta = \beta - B \tag{4b}$$

$$d = \epsilon + \delta \tag{5a}$$
$$\therefore d = (a - \alpha) + (\alpha - A)$$
$$= a - A \tag{5b}$$

Basic assumptions

$$r_{\alpha\epsilon} = r_{\beta\omega} = r_{\alpha\omega} = r_{\beta\epsilon} = 0 \tag{6a}$$

$$r_{\epsilon\omega} = 0 \tag{6b}$$

$$r_{A\epsilon} = r_{B\omega} = r_{A\omega} = r_{B\epsilon} = 0 \tag{6c}$$

Scaling

$$\bar{\epsilon} = \bar{\omega} = 0 \tag{7}$$

Appendix B

It follows from formula 1a that

$$\bar{a} = \bar{\alpha} + \bar{\epsilon} \quad (8a)$$
$$\bar{b} = \bar{\beta} + \bar{\omega} \quad (8b)$$

From 7 and 8 it follows that

$$\bar{a} = \bar{\alpha} \quad (9a)$$
$$\bar{b} = \bar{\beta} \quad (9b)$$

From 4a it follows that

$$\begin{aligned} r_{\delta\epsilon} &= r_{(\alpha-A)\epsilon} \\ &= \frac{r_{\alpha\epsilon}\sigma_\alpha\sigma_\epsilon - r_{A\epsilon}\sigma_A\sigma_\epsilon}{\sigma_\delta\sigma_\epsilon} \\ &= 0 \end{aligned} \quad (10)$$

Notation referring to "accuracy analogues:"

λ_{aa} = coefficient of accuracy for test A
  = "accuracy analogue" of reliability coefficient r_{aa}
λ_a = "accuracy analogue" of σ_a
λ_{ab} = "accuracy analogue" of correlation coefficient r_{ab}
λ_{a-A} = "accuracy analogue" of standard error of measurement $\sigma_{a-\alpha}$

Definitions of accuracy analogues:

> An accuracy analogue of a statistic is the statistic obtained by substituting A for α and $\bar{A}$ *for* $\bar{a}$ *or for* $\bar{\alpha}$.

Thus, since

$$\begin{aligned} r_{aa} &= 1 - \frac{\sigma_{a-\alpha}^2}{\sigma_a^2} \\ &= 1 - \frac{\Sigma(a-\alpha)^2}{N} \bigg/ \frac{\Sigma(a-\bar{a})^2}{N} \end{aligned} \quad (11a)$$

it follows that

$$\lambda_{aa} = 1 - \frac{\Sigma(a-A)^2}{N} \bigg/ \frac{\Sigma(a-\bar{A})^2}{N} \quad (11b)$$

Since
$$\sigma_a = \sqrt{\frac{\Sigma(a - \bar{a})^2}{N}} \qquad (12a)$$

it follows that
$$\lambda_a = \sqrt{\frac{\Sigma(a - \bar{A})^2}{N}} \qquad (12b)$$

Since
$$r_{ab} = \frac{\Sigma(a - \bar{a})(b - \bar{b})}{N\sigma_a\sigma_b} \qquad (13a)$$

it follows that
$$\lambda_{ab} = \frac{\Sigma(a - \bar{A})(b - \bar{B})}{N\lambda_a\lambda_b} \qquad (13b)$$

Formula 11 for test A becomes:

$$\lambda_{aa} = 1 - \frac{\Sigma(a - A)^2/N}{\Sigma(a - \bar{A})^2/N} \qquad (14)$$

$$= 1 - \frac{\Sigma d^2/N}{\sigma_a^2 + (\bar{a} - \bar{A})^2}$$

$$= 1 - \frac{\sigma_d^2 + \bar{d}^2}{\sigma_a^2 + \bar{d}^2} \qquad (15)$$

$$\sigma_d^2 = \sigma_{\epsilon+\delta}^2$$
$$= \sigma_\epsilon^2 + \sigma_\delta^2 + 2r_{\delta\epsilon}\sigma_\epsilon\sigma_\delta \qquad (16)$$

Since
$$r_{\delta\epsilon} = 0 \qquad (10)$$
$$\sigma_d^2 = \sigma_\epsilon^2 + \sigma_\delta^2 \qquad (17)$$

From (5a) it follows that

$$\bar{d} = \bar{\epsilon} + \bar{\delta} \qquad (18)$$

Appendix B

Since
$$\bar{\epsilon} = 0 \tag{7}$$
$$\bar{d} = \bar{\delta} \tag{19}$$

Substituting (17) and (19) into (15):

$$\lambda_{aa} = 1 - \frac{\sigma_\epsilon^2 + \bar{\bar{\delta}}^2 + \sigma_\delta^2}{\sigma_a^2 + \bar{\bar{\delta}}^2} \tag{20}$$

$$r_{aa} = 1 - \frac{\sigma_\epsilon^2}{\sigma_a^2} \tag{21}$$

Comparing (20) and (21) we see that:

$$r_{aa} \geq \lambda_{aa} \tag{22}$$

The standard error of measurement of scores on test A is

$$\sigma_{a \cdot \alpha} = \sigma_{a-\alpha} = \sigma_\epsilon \tag{23}$$
$$= \sigma_a \sqrt{1 - r_{aa}} \tag{24}$$

(The derivation of formula 24 is not presented here; it is well known and can be found in many standard textbooks on statistics.)

The accuracy analogue of the standard error of measurement is

$$\lambda_{a-A} = \sqrt{\frac{\Sigma [(a - A) - (\bar{A} - \bar{A})]^2}{N}}$$

$$= \sqrt{\frac{\Sigma (a - A)^2}{N}}$$

$$= \sqrt{\frac{\Sigma d^2}{N}}$$

$$= \sqrt{\sigma_d^2 + \bar{d}^2} \tag{25}$$

Substituting formulas 17 and 19 in 25:

$$\lambda_{a-A} = \sqrt{\sigma_\epsilon^2 + \sigma_\delta^2 + \bar{\bar{\delta}}^2} \tag{26}$$

Modified accuracy analogues (λ') are approximations of the accuracy analogues (λ). The approximation procedure consists in assuming that δ is constant, that is, equal for all values of α, and that therefore:

$$\sigma_\delta = 0 \qquad (27)$$

Substituting (27) in (20), to get the formula for λ'_{aa}

$$\lambda_{aa} = 1 - \frac{\sigma_\epsilon^2 + \bar{\delta}^2}{\sigma_a^2 + \bar{\delta}^2} \qquad (28)$$

Comparing (20) and (28) we see that λ'_{aa} is an upper-bound estimate of λ_{aa}

$$\lambda'_{aa} \geq \lambda_{aa} \qquad (29)$$

Comparing (21) and (28) we see that

$$r_{aa} \geq \lambda'_{aa} \qquad (30)$$

Combining (29) and (30):

$$r_{aa} \geq \lambda'_{aa} \geq \lambda_{aa} \qquad (31)$$

Note that the procedure for correcting reliability coefficients (r_{aa}) for range applies also to the analogue λ'_{aa} (though not to λ_{aa}).

The formula for correcting r_{aa} for range is:

$$r_{aa(2)} = 1 - \frac{\sigma_{a(1)}^2}{\sigma_{a(2)}^2}[1 - r_{aa(1)}] \qquad (32)$$

where the subscripts 1 and 2 in parentheses indicate the sample on which the statistic is based.

Appendix B

It can readily be shown that the corresponding formula for correcting λ'_{aa} for range applies. The formula is:

$$\lambda'_{aa(2)} = 1 - \frac{{\lambda'_{a(1)}}^2}{{\lambda'_{a(2)}}^2}[1 - \lambda'_{aa(1)}] \tag{33}$$

The derivation of formula 33 is analogous to that used by Kelley (1947, pp. 426–27) in deriving formula 32 (Formula 11:46a, in Kelley's derivation).

The modified accuracy analogue of the standard error of measurement is obtained by substituting (27) in (26)

$$\lambda'_{a-A} = \sqrt{\sigma_\epsilon^2 + \overline{\bar{\delta}^2}} \tag{34}$$

$$= \sqrt{\sigma_{a \cdot \alpha}^2 + \overline{\bar{\delta}^2}} \tag{35}$$

Other standard formulas, too, have analogues of the λ type. Table B-2 (on pages 162–163) summarizes them. Their algebraic derivations, which are not presented here, are for the most part quite obvious to those familiar with the derivation of the corresponding standard formula.

Table B-2. Standard Formulas (for Conventional Statistics) and Corresponding Formulas for Statistics Referring to or Dependent on Absolute Scores.

	Standard formula		Corresponding absolute-score formula	
Standard deviation	$\sigma_a = \sqrt{\dfrac{\sum(a - \bar{a})^2}{N}}$	(12a)	$\lambda_a = \sqrt{\dfrac{\sum(a - \bar{A})^2}{N}}$	(12b)
Correlation coefficient	$r_{ab} = \dfrac{\sum(a - \bar{a})(b - \bar{b})}{N \sigma_a \sigma_b}$	(13a)	$\lambda_{ab} = \dfrac{\sum(a - \bar{A})(b - \bar{B})}{N \lambda_a \lambda_b}$	(13b)
Reliability coefficient	$r_{aa} = \dfrac{\sigma_\alpha^2}{\sigma_a^2}$	(36a)	$\lambda'_{aa} = \dfrac{\lambda'^2_A}{\lambda_a^2}$	(36b)
Reliability index (correlation between obtained score and true score on a test)	$r_{a\alpha} = \dfrac{\sigma_\alpha}{\sigma_a}$	(37a)	$\lambda'_{aA} = \dfrac{\lambda'_A}{\lambda_a}$	(37b)
	$= \sqrt{r_{aa}}$	(38a)	$= \sqrt{\lambda'_{aa}}$	(38b)
Standard error of measurement	$\sigma_{a \cdot \alpha} = \sigma_a \sqrt{1 - r_{aa}}$	(24)	$\lambda_{a-A} = \sqrt{\sigma_\epsilon^2 + \sigma_\delta^2 + \overline{\delta^2}}$	(26)

Appendix B

Correction of reliability coefficient for range	$r_{aa(2)} = 1 - \dfrac{\sigma_{a(1)}^2}{\sigma_{a(2)}^2}[1 - r_{aa(1)}]$	(32)	$\lambda'_{aa(2)} = 1 - \dfrac{\lambda_{a(1)}^2}{\lambda_{a(2)}^2}[1 - \lambda'_{aa(1)}]$	(33)
Correction of correlation for attenuation	$r_{ab} = r_{ab}/\sqrt{r_{aa}}$	(39a)	$\lambda_{ab} = \lambda_{ab}/\sqrt{\lambda'_{aa}}$	(39b)
Variance of a sum	$\sigma_{a+b}^2 = \sigma_a^2 + \sigma_b^2 + 2r_{ab}\sigma_a\sigma_b$	(40a)	$\lambda_{a+b}^2 = \lambda_a^2 + \lambda_b^2 + 2\lambda_{ab}\lambda_a\lambda_b$	(40b)
Variance of a difference	$\sigma_{a-b}^2 = \sigma_a^2 + \sigma_b^2 - 2r_{ab}\sigma_a\sigma_b$	(41a)	$\lambda_{a-b}^2 = \lambda_a^2 + \lambda_b^2 - 2\lambda_{ab}\lambda_a\lambda_b$	(41b)

Index

Absolute-meaning metric, 76
Accuracy, 94–98; *see also* Accuracy analogue(s); Accuracy analogue statistics
  concept of, 94
Accuracy analogue(s), 155-163
  concept of, 155
  correction of attenuation, 162
  correction for range, 160–161
  definition of, 157
  of standard error of measurement, 159
  modified, 160
Accuracy analogue statistics, 95
  basic assumptions of, 156
  basic formulas for, 156
  standard statistics and, 95–98, 157–163
  table of formulas for, 162
  usefulness of, 98
Accuracy coefficient
  compared with Livingston's coefficient, 96
  random and systematic error and, 96–97
  reliability coefficient and, 95–98
  usefulness of, 98
Achievement test(s)
  compared with aptitude tests, 9–11
  content and correlation validity for, 92
  criterion-referenced tests and, 9, 10
  norm-referenced tests and, 9, 10
Angoff, W. H., 11, 13, 89–90, 118
Angoff formula for reliability, 89–90
Aptitude tests, 9–11; *see also* Predictive test(s)

Baker, E. L., 28, 111, 120
Behavioral objectives, *see also* Objectives
  criterion-referenced tests and, 17
  educational objectives and, 26–28
  fallacies about, 109
  goal and measurement components of, 24–25
  indicators and, 24–25
  objective-referenced tests and, 22–25
  sampling and, 35–37
Binomial distribution role in distribution of scores, 124–126, 150

Carver, R. P., 83, 85, 118
Chall, J., 31, 119
Chance
  correcting for, 76–78
  guessing and, 77
Choice-weighted scoring, 79
Classical psychometric theory, 80–83, 105, 124
Coefficient of accuracy, *see* Accuracy coefficient
Competence level, 66, 122
  cutting scores and, 148–153
  stage of instruction and, 150
  standards, 65–70, 122–124; *see also* Standards of competence
Computer-constructed tests, 48-49
Constructed answer tests, 38
  theoretical distribution of scores for, 128–131
Content standard tests, 7

Index

Correction-for-chance formula, 77
  choice-weighted scoring vs., 79
Correction for attenuation, 162
Criterion-referenced measurement,
      see also Criterion-referenced
      tests
  common misconceptions of, 1
  definition of, 3–5
  norm-referenced measurement
      vs., 3
  objective-referenced measurement
      vs., 2
  types of, 2, 4
Criterion-referenced tests, *see also*
      Domain-referenced tests;
      Objective-referenced tests
  and accuracy, 94–98
  accuracy analogue statistics and,
      155
  achievement tests and, 9, 10
  behavioral objectives and, 17
  chance and multiple-choice, 76–77
  classical psychometric theory and,
      83
  data needed for evaluation of, 85
  diagnostic tests and, 6
  domain-referenced measurement
      vs., 2
  domain tests and, 7
  evaluation of
    pretest and posttest scores in, 86
    validity and, 91–94
  evaluation of educational programs
      and validity of, 93
  fallacies about, 105–108
    in relation to norm-referenced
        tests, 103
  history of, 5–8
    concept and term in, 6, 7
  how to use norms for, 59–60
  importance of test item analysis
      for, 50–54
  mastery level vs. standard of
      competence for, 69

Criterion-referenced tests (*cont'd.*)
  non-paper-and-pencil, 13
  norm-referenced tests vs., 9–11,
      17, 50–54
    chief differences of, 53–54
  norms for
    how to develop, 56–58
    need for, 56
  objective-referenced tests vs.,
      13–15
  posttest and pretest scores in, 82
  predictive tests and, 10–11
  predictive validity and, 93–94
  psychometric and edumetric
      procedures in, 83–84
  rationale for, 28–29
  reliability of, 86–91
  sampling from domain and, 29
  standard test theory and evaluation
      of, 80–81
  standardized tests as antecedent
      of, 5–6
  utility of, 7, 8, 61–65
    for comparison of instructional
        approaches, 63
    for evaluation of change, 65
    for evaluation of individuals with
        respect to a domain, 64
    for evaluation of instructional
        approach, 63
    for evaluation of program or
        curriculum, 75–76
    for evaluation of status, 61
    for evaluation of students, 62
    for formative evaluations, 74–75
    for placement of students, 63
    for summative evaluations,
        75–76
  variability and reliability of, 88
Cutting score(s), 66–67, 70–71,
      122–154
  educational importance of,
      153–154
  false failures and, 150–153

Cutting score(s) (*cont'd.*)
 false passes and, 126, 150–153
 levels of competence and, 148–153
 misclassification and, 126, 150–153
 optimum, 150, 153
 paradoxical results and, 71, 153
 relation to standard of competence, 65–66, 70–71
 sampling errors and, 71
 setting, 70–71, 123, 126, 148–153
 stage of instruction and, 151–153

Davis, F. B., 38, 69, 79, 118
Diagnostic tests, 6
Diamond, J. J., 38, 69, 118
Dillman, F. E., Jr., 111, 118
Displacement of score scale, 124
Domain
 criterion-referenced tests and sampling from, 29
 defining a, 19–22
 population of, 21
 repeated testing and, 72–74
 sampling from, 29–37
  formal, 35–37
 standard of competence, 65–67
 units constituting, 20–21
Domain-referenced measurement, *see also* Domain-referenced tests
 criterion-referenced measurement vs., 2
 definition of, 4
 objective-referenced measurement vs., 2, 4, 5
Domain-referenced tests, 7, 15–16
 content standard tests and, 7
 criterion-referenced tests and, 37–45
 defining domain for, 19–22; *see also* Domain
 difficulty and specificity of test items in multiple-choice, 39–42

Domain-referenced tests (*cont'd.*)
 individual and group norms in, 59–60
 information provided by, 15, 16
 objective-referenced tests vs., 15, 59–60
 stratified sampling procedure in, 30–34
 test item analysis for, 50–51
 vocabulary test as example of, 19–22
  difficulty in writing items for, 42–43
 rationale for, 30–34, 46–47
 writing multiple-choice test items for, 38–42
Domain tests, 7

Ebel, R. L., 7–8, 83, 118
Educational objectives
 behavioral objectives and, 26–28
 teaching to the test and, 26
 ultimate objectives vs., 28
Edumetric procedures, 85–86
Error(s) of measurement, *see also* Chance; Guessing
 cutting scores and classificatory, 150–153
 definition of, 123
 displacement of score scale and, 124
 random, 123–124
 standard
  formula for accuracy analogue of, 159
  modified accuracy analogues and, 161
  notation for accuracy analogue of, 157
 systematic, 123–124
Evaluation(s)
 accuracy and, 94–98
 of criterion-referenced tests, 80–82
 data needed for, 85

Index

Evaluation(s) (*cont'd.*)
  posttest and pretest scores in, 82
  standard test theory and, 80–81
  formative, 74–75
  pretest and posttest scores in, 82, 86
  summative, 75–76
  validity and, 91–94
    educational programs and, 93

Fallacies of testing, table of, 103–110
Flanagan, J. C., 6–7, 28, 54, 112, 118, 119
Formative evaluations, 74–75

Geis, G. L., 111, 119
Glaser, R., 6–7, 119
Grade-equivalent norms, 57–58
Gronlund, N. E., 111, 119
Guessing, 76–78, 100
  binomial distribution and, 124, 126
  multiple-choice tests and, 124, 126

Hively, W., 48, 119
Horst, D. P., 3, 58, 98, 119, 120
Husek, T. R., 80–81, 88, 98, 120
Hypothetical distributions, binomial distributions and, 150

Indicator, *see* Behavioral objectives
Item analysis
  for domain-referenced tests, 50–51
  importance of internal consistency in, 53
  for objective-referenced tests, 51–53
  posttest situation and, 54
Item form, 48; *see also* Standardized item format
Item shell, 48–49, *see also* Standardized item format
Item writing, 37–49

Kelley, T. L., 119, 161
Kuder-Richardson formula for reliability, 89–90

Levels of competence, *see* Competence level
Lindquist, E. F., 26–27, 119
Livingston, S. A., 90–91, 96, 116, 119
Livingston's reliability coefficient
  coefficient of accuracy and, 96
  method of computing, 90–91
Lorge, I., 15, 21, 31, 119, 120

Mager, R. F., 28, 111, 119
Mastery level
  concept of, 69–70
  cutting score and, 153
  measurement of, 22, 37
  objectives and, 69
  paradoxical results and, 153
  standard of competence vs., 69
Mattson, D. E., 11, 120
Measurement, error(s) of
  chance and, 76–77
  cutting scores and classificatory, 150–153
  definition of, 123
  displacement of score scale and, 124
  guessing and, 77–78, 124, 126
  random, 123–124
  standard, *see* Standard error of measurement
  systematic, 123–124
Millman, J., xv
Multiple-choice tests, 38
  binomial distribution of scores on, 124, 126
  correcting for chance for, 76–79
  formula for, 77
  fallacies about, 110
  guessing and, 124–126; *see also* Chance
  scoring, 76–79

Index

Multiple-choice tests (*cont'd.*)
  theoretical distribution of scores for, 128–147
    for constructed item tests, 128–131
    for five-choice item tests, 132–135
    for four-choice item tests, 136–139
    for three-choice item tests, 140–143
    for two-choice item tests, 144–147
  writing test items for, 38–42

Nitko, A. J., 48, 120
Norm-referenced measurement, 1, 3, 11, 17, 100–101, 103–105; *see also* Norm-referenced tests
Norm-referenced tests, 3
  criterion-referenced tests vs., 11–13, 17, 50–53, 67–68
  fallacies about, 1, 103–104
Norms
  for criterion-referenced tests, 56–60
    how to develop, 56–58
    how to use, 59–60
    need for, 56
  definition of, 6
  individual and group, 59–60
  kinds of, 57
  problems of grade-equivalent, 57–58
  setting standard of competence and, 67–68

Objective-referenced measurement, *see also* Objective referenced tests
  criterion-referenced measurement vs., 2
  definition of, 4

Object-referenced (*cont'd.*)
  domain, referenced measurement vs., 2, 4, 5
Objective-referenced tests, 13–15
  behavioral objectives and, 22–25
  defining objectives for, 22–28
    minimum standards in, 23–24
  dichotomous vs. continuous score scale in, 13–15
  domain-referenced tests vs., 59–60
  individual and group norms in, 59–60
  test item analysis for, 51–53
Objectives, *see also* Behavioral objectives
  defining, for objective-referenced tests, 22–28
  difficulty in measuring, 25
  indicators vs., 24–25
  mastery level and, 69
  measurement and, 54
  sampling, 35–37
  standards vs., 23–24
  ultimate, 27–28
    educational objectives vs., 28
  validation of, 26

Popham, W. J., 28, 80–81, 88, 98, 111, 120
Predictive tests, 9–11, 109; *see also* Aptitude tests
Predictive validity, 93–94
Prognostic tests, 6
Psychometric procedures, 85–86
Psychometric theory, classical, 83, 105, 124

Random error, 123–124; *see also* Chance
Rationales, *see* Test rationales
Raw score, 76
References, 118–121
Reliability, 86–91
  computing, 89–90

Reliability (*cont'd.*)
    criticism of Livingston method of, 90–91
    variability and, 88
Reliability coefficient
    accuracy analogue for, 162
    Angoff formula 16, 89–90
    coefficient of accuracy and, 95–98
    formula for correcting, 160
        for range, 162
    Kuder-Richardson, 89–90
    Spearman-Brown, 89
    split-half, 89–90
Reliability index, 162
Repeated testing
    domain and, 72–74
    handling, 72–73
    need for, 72
    sampling and, 72–74
    teaching-to-the-test problem and, 74
Richards, J. M., Jr., 48–49, 120

Sampling, *see also* Domain
    behavioral objectives and, 35–36
    from domain, 29–37
    in domain-referenced tests vs. objective-referenced tests, 35–36
    errors and cutting score, 71
    errors and stratification in, 33
    formal, 29, 35–37
        random, 35–36
    repeated testing and, 72–74
    stratified, 30–34
        random, 36
Scholastic Aptitude Test (SAT), 10–11
Score(s), 122
    binomial distribution of, 124, 126
    calculating theoretical distribution of, 127
    cutting, *see* Cutting score(s)

Score(s) (*cont'd*)
    guessing and, 124–126; *see also* Chance
    raw, 76
    theoretical distribution of, tabulated for multiple-choice tests, 132–149
Scoring, 76–79, 110
Shaycoft, M. S., 7, 54, 99, 120, 154
Split-half reliability coefficient, 89–90
Stage of instruction
    competence level and, 150
    cutting scores and, 151–152
        percentage of misclassifications and, 151
        relative amount of misclassifications and, 152
Standard(s)
    definition of, 6
    objectives vs., 23–24
Standard deviation, formula and accuracy analogue for, 162
Standard error of measurement
    accuracy analogue for, 162
    formula for, 159
        modified, 161
        notation for, 157
    formula for, 159, 162
Standard of competence, 65–70, 122–124,
    concept of, 65–67
    cutting score vs., 70
    experience vs. formal research in setting, 68
    mastery level vs., 69
    norms and setting, 67–68
Standard test theory, 80–81; *see also* Classical psychometric theory
Standardized item format, *see* Item shell
Standardized tests, 5–6
Stratified sampling procedure, *see* Sampling, stratified

Index

Summative evaluations, 75–76
Survey tests, 6
Systematic error, 123–124

Tallmadge, G. K., 3, 58, 98, 119, 120
Teaching to the test, 26, 74
Test(s)
  achievement, 92
  categories of norm-referenced, 6
  classification of, 12
  constructed-answer, 38
  criterion-referenced, *see*
    Criterion-referenced tests
  diagnostic, 6
  domain-referenced, *see*
    Domain-referenced tests
  evaluation of; *see also* Accuracy,
    Reliability, and Validity
    data needed for, 85
    pretest and posttest scores in, 86
  multiple-choice, 38
    fallacies about, 110
  non-paper-and-pencil, 13
  norm-referenced, *see*
    Norm-referenced tests
  objective-referenced, *see*
    Objective-referenced tests
  predictive, fallacies about, 109
  purpose and type of, 17–18
  reliability of, 86–91
  scoring multiple-choice, 76–79
  standard theory of, 80–81
  standardized, 5–6
  theoretical distribution of scores
    for
    constructed-answer, 128–131
    multiple-choice, 127
    tabulated for multiple-choice,
      132–149
  tryout, 50–54
  validity and, 91–94
  variability and reliability of, 88
Test items
  constructed-answer vs.
    multiple-choice, 38
  difficulty and specificity of, 39–42
  difficulty in writing, for vocabulary
    test, 42–45
  importance of writer experience
    for, 49
  standardized item format for
    writing, 48–49
  test rationales and, 29, 37–49
  writing multiple-choice, 38–42
Test rationales, 28–29
Testing
  fallacies about, 103–110
  repeated, *see* Repeated testing
Theoretical distribution of scores
  calculating method for, 127
  for constructed-answer tests,
    128–131
  for multiple-choice tests, 132–149
    with five-choice items, 132–135
    with four-choice items, 136–139
    with three-choice items, 140–143
    with two-choice items, 144–147
Thorndike, E. L., 15, 21, 31, 120, 121
Typical child, concept of, 68

Universe of items, *see* Domain

Validity, 91–94
  correlation and content, 92
  definition of, 93
  external criterion and content,
    91–92
  predictive, 93–94
Variance
  formula and accuracy analogue for,
    162
  reliability and, 88
Vocabulary tests
  definitions in, 42–45
  diagrams vs. definitions in, 43–45
  difficulties in writing items for,
    42–43

Vocabulary tests (*cont'd.*)
  as example of defining domain for domain-referenced test, 19–22
  as example of difficulties in constructing criterion-referenced tests, 45–47
  as example of rationale for domain-referenced test, 30–34
  as example of stratified sampling procedure, 30–34
  as example of writing multiple-choice test items, 39–42

Vocabulary tests (*cont'd.*)
  examples of item shell for, 48–49
  examples vs. definitions in, 43
  form of word in, 44
  multimeaning words in, 42
  test rationale tabulated for domain-referenced, 46–47
  thesaurus categories in, 42

Warrington, W. G., 11, 13–14, 121
Wight, A. R., 23, 24–25, 121
Wood, C. T., 3, 58, 98, 119

LIBRARY OF DAVIDSON COLLEGE